English ⌗ Heritage

Guide to English Heritage Properties

Over 350 Places to Visit in 1992

The Gatehouse of Battle Abbey, East Sussex.
The Gatehouse is open to the public for the first time in 1992, and includes a major new exhibition.

Front cover: Boscobel House, Shropshire (see page 122). After being defeated by Parliament's army at the Battle of Worcester in 1651, the future King Charles II sought refuge from the Roundheads here at what was then a remote hunting lodge. 1992 marks the 350th anniversary of the outbreak of the Civil War. (English Heritage Photographic Section.)

Back cover (from top, left to right): English Heritage conservators at Audley End House, Essex; carriage rides at Osborne House, Isle of Wight; the gardens of Chiswick House, London; the parlour of Boscobel House, Shropshire; Richmond Castle, North Yorkshire; the English Civil War Society in action at an English Heritage Special Event.

Copyright © English Heritage 1992
First published 1985
Eighth (revised) edition published 1992

Edited by Mark Lawrence
Designed by Momentum Sales Promotion and Design Ltd, London NW6
Printed in England by William Clowes Ltd., Beccles, Suffolk

C1620 2/92

ISBN 1 85074 370 3

CONTENTS ⬚

Handing on our History _____ 4

Working to Preserve the Past _____ 5

English Heritage Membership _____ 6-7

Opening Times & Prices _____ 8

Planning your Route _____ 9

Visitor Facilities _____ 10

Events & Concerts 1992 _____ 11

Useful Addresses _____ 12

Map of English Counties _____ 13

County by County Guide

Avon _____ 14-15

Bedfordshire _____ 16-17

Berkshire _____ 18

Cambridgeshire _____ 19-20

Cheshire _____ 21-22

Cleveland _____ 23

Cornwall _____ 24-28

Cumbria _____ 29-34

Derbyshire _____ 35-37

Devon _____ 38-42

Dorset _____ 43-45

Durham _____ 46-47

Essex _____ 48-50

Gloucestershire _____ 51-54

Greater London _____ 55-59

Hadrian's Wall _____ 60-65

Hampshire _____ 66-72

Hereford and Worcester _____ 73-75

Hertfordshire _____ 76

Humberside _____ 77-78

Isle of Wight _____ 79-81

Isles of Scilly _____ 82-83

Kent _____ 84-91

Lancashire _____ 92-93

Leicestershire _____ 94-95

Lincolnshire _____ 96-97

Norfolk _____ 98-102

Northamptonshire _____ 103-104

Northumberland _____ 105-109

North Yorkshire _____ 110-116

Nottinghamshire _____ 117

Oxfordshire _____ 118-120

Shropshire _____ 121-125

Somerset _____ 126-128

South Yorkshire _____ 129-130

Staffordshire _____ 131-132

Suffolk _____ 133-135

Surrey _____ 136-137

Sussex (East & West)_____ 138-140

Tyne and Wear _____ 141-142

Warwickshire _____ 143-144

West Midlands _____ 145

Wiltshire _____ 146-151

Index _____ 152-156

Deed of Covenant and
Direct Debit Forms _____ 157

Membership Application Form _____ 159

3

HANDING ON OUR HISTORY

THE PRESENCE of England's rich history is to be seen everywhere in the great wealth of monuments, buildings and other architectural treasures from our past. It is a major national task to protect and preserve this legacy, and hand it on for future generations to understand and enjoy. English Heritage is the independent public body created by Parliament in 1984 to carry out this task.

Over 350 historic properties throughout England are in the guardianship of English Heritage, from prehistoric and Roman remains, to imposing medieval castles and abbeys, great stately homes and working industrial monuments. The entire portfolio of buildings and monuments in our care are featured in this Guide, whether they are world famous landmarks like Stonehenge or Hadrian's Wall, or quieter, more atmospheric historic buildings off the beaten track, such as Stokesay Castle and Mount Grace Priory.

We aim to share this unique aspect of our nation's history by making a visit to an English Heritage property an enjoyable and educational experience, not only through the lively exhibitions, museums and personal stereo guided tours available at many properties, but also through our extensive programme of carefully researched historical re-enactments, displays, concerts and other special events.

Stonehenge

WORKING TO PRESERVE THE PAST

MEMBERSHIP OF English Heritage offers free admission to all the properties that we manage. But just as importantly, membership is a personal contribution to the preservation and protection of *all* England's architectural heritage, from the humble red telephone box to our grandest cathedrals, from ancient archaeological sites to our most beautiful historic towns. Although partly funded by Government grants, the continuing success of our work relies on subscriptions from our members, whose numbers are ever growing.

Westminster Abbey Chapter House

Over half a million historic buildings in England, whether privately owned, managed by local authorities or other conservation bodies, such as the National Trust, are now protected by law from thoughtless demolition or alteration through having been listed. English Heritage advises Government on which buildings warrant listing and what alterations should be permitted. We can offer repair grants ranging from a few thousand pounds to as much as £1 million for major conservation projects, such as the Ribblehead Viaduct in Yorkshire. And recent Government legislation now means that, for the first time, we are also able to offer grants for the repair and maintenance of England's great cathedrals.

English Heritage also plans to schedule some 60,000 of our most important ancient monuments and archaeological sites in order to protect them by law. Our archaeologists carry out rescue excavations to ensure that we learn as much as we can from those ancient sites that are soon to be destroyed by city development, road building, farming or quarrying.

As well as archaeologists, our permanent staff also includes architects, art historians, craftsmen such as ironsmiths, stonecarvers, and painting restorers, and others. They all use their skills to conserve our important monuments, buildings and the treasures they contain, and help English Heritage to preserve, protect and hand on to future generations the nation's great architectural legacy.

5

JOIN US TODAY

PRESERVING, restoring, excavating and rescuing our built heritage requires an enormous financial commitment. But as the pressures on our historic environment increase, we need to respond with even greater urgency.

This is why we need your help. By becoming a member of English Heritage you will be helping us to continue our essential work.

As a member you will enjoy many valuable benefits:

- Free admission to all English Heritage properties.
- Free or reduced admission to the many special events and concerts held at our properties.
- Reduced admission fees to many historic sites in Wales and Scotland and the Jorvik Viking Centre in York.
- A Member's Pack with *Guide to English Heritage Properties*, Map, Events Diary, car sticker and badges.
- *English Heritage Magazine* sent to you quarterly.
- The opportunity to join special cruises and tours for members.

Join immediately, when you visit any staffed English Heritage property, or complete the application form on page 159.

Please consider covenanting your subscription and paying by direct debit, which will enable you to contribute much more to English Heritage through your subscription at no extra cost to yourself. There are Direct Debit and Deed of Covenant forms on page 157 to make this easy for you

Join us today, help us continue our work and discover the benefits of English Heritage membership.

MOBIL IN THE UK

MOBIL HAS BEEN sponsoring events throughout the UK for over 15 years. The arts, sport, architectural heritage and environmental projects all have a place in our extensive portfolio. The company concentrates its activities in areas where it has many customers or a large number of employees. In this way, people all over the country can benefit from our sponsorships.

Arts sponsorships include annual concerts in Greenwich, Southend, Manchester, Birkenhead and Lichfield, exhibitions and theatrical projects. Mobil Touring Theatre regularly takes top quality productions of well-known plays to venues all over the country, while the Mobil Playwriting Competition, run jointly with the Royal Exchange Theatre in Manchester, gives new plays and their writers a chance to achieve international recognition.

Mobil has sponsored guides to the Victoria and Albert Museum and to the three London houses administered by the V & A: Apsley House, Osterley Park and Ham House. On Merseyside, where it has a large blending plant, Mobil has co-funded restoration projects in Birkenhead Park and in Birkenhead Town Hall, and supports the Liverpool Festival of Comedy.

Sports sponsorships vary from international athletics and motorsport to youth sport at a local level. For example, Mobil Matchplay is an annual cricket tournament for young cricketers in Essex, where Mobil has a large refinery.

The company has also funded an Essex County Cricket Club cricket training video for young people and coaches.

One of the company's recent ventures is the Mobil Greensight Pack, an environmental video project for schoolchildren created in conjunction with Living Earth and The Green Alliance.

English ⌗ Heritage

Use your membership throughout Britain

Edinburgh Castle.

If you're planning a trip to Scotland or Wales this year don't forget to take your English Heritage Membership card with you. It entitles you to free entry (half price in your first year of membership) to over 100 historic properties in the care of Historic Scotland and Cadw: Welsh Historic Monuments.

We've also arranged for our members to enjoy reduced price admission to the Jorvik Viking Centre in York, one of England's most popular historic attractions.

All the properties in the care of our sister organisations are marked on your Map of English Heritage Properties. For more details please phone Historic Scotland on 031-244 3101, Welsh Historic Monuments on (0222) 465511 or Jorvik Viking Centre on (0904) 643211.

OPENING TIMES

ALMOST ALL staffed properties follow the same pattern of opening, indicated after the symbol ☉ by the conventions 'All year' or 'Summer season'. The few exceptions to these times as stated below are noted against individual properties.

All Year
Good Friday or 1 April (whichever is earlier) to 30 September: Open daily 10am-6pm
and
1 October to Maundy Thursday or 31 March (whichever is earlier): Open Tuesday-Sunday 10am-4pm; Closed 24-26 December and 1 January.

Summer Season
Good Friday or 1 April (whichever is earlier) to 30 September: Open daily 10am-6pm.

Please note that outside the summer season many properties are closed on Mondays.

Lunchtime Closing
Many properties otherwise open for the normal hours may close for lunch, usually 1-2pm. Telephone the property or its Area Office (see page 12) to check before your visit.

Closing at Short Notice
It is sometimes necessary to close a property for odd days at short notice, for instance for staff training, but this is usually only during the winter season. To avoid disappointment, telephone the property or its Area Office (see page 12) to check before your visit.

Keykeeper
Where indicated in the listings, to gain access to a property, a key must be obtained from a keykeeper, who usually lives locally. Details are usually displayed at the property itself but can be obtained in advance of your visit by contacting the relevant Area Office (see page 12).

ADMISSION PRICES

ALL ADMISSION PRICES given in this Guide come into effect on 1 April 1992 and are current until 31 March 1993. Admission to all properties is free to members of English Heritage.

There is no admission charge unless shown in the listings. For such properties, prices are listed, for example, £1.10/85p/55p. These, respectively, are the charges for: Adults; Senior Citizens, the unemployed (on production of a UB40) and students (on production of a student union card); Children under 16 (children under 5 are admitted free).

There may be an increased admission charge for non-members on days when a special event is being held at a property.

Group Discounts

A discount of 15% is given on admission charges for groups of 11 or more at most English Heritage properties. At Stonehenge a 10% discount is given. Accompanying Group Leaders are admitted free.

Student Groups and School Parties

These are admitted free to English Heritage properties, but should book in advance through the relevant Area Office (see page 12).

The National Trust

Some properties, marked (NT), are maintained and run by English Heritage but owned by the National Trust. Members of both organisations are admitted free of charge.

HOW TO GET THERE

DIRECTIONS on where to find each property by road are given in each listing, including the National Grid and Ordnance Survey map reference.

Bus and Rail

Where access to a property by public transport is possible, details are given. All buses providing access to a property are shown and, unless otherwise stated, pass the entrance. A nil entry for a bus implies there is no reasonable service. The nearest railway station is shown, but sometimes an alternative is added, either where the closer has a poor service or the other is on a different line.

English Heritage is grateful to Mr. Barry S. Doe for the public transport information. He will welcome and acknowledge letters from anyone finding errors or suggesting improvements. Please write to him at: Travadvice, 25 Newmorton Road, Moordown, Bournemouth, Dorset BH9 3NU (Tel: (0202) 528707).

Car Parking

This is available at or near properties marked **P**. For many properties where the parking symbol is not given, it is nevertheless possible to park easily and safely nearby. There is no charge for parking unless specified for a property.

VISITOR FACILITIES

Souvenir Guides and Handbooks

At properties marked 🗋, a fully illustrated colour souvenir guide is available. For a full catalogue of English Heritage publications and details of how to order, please write to English Heritage Postal Sales, PO Box 229, Northamptonshire NN6 9RY.

Personal Stereo Tours

These lively and informative guides are available at selected properties. Where you see the symbol 🎧 the tour is included in the admission charge. The symbol 🎧 indicates that the tour is available at the additional cost of £1.00.

Education Centres

At properties marked 🗒 an Education Centre has been provided for study use by school parties. These are equipped with audio visual, printed and replica sources appropriate to the property, which teachers can use themselves. Education Centres can be booked in advance. For more information, please contact the English Heritage Education Service, Keysign House, 429 Oxford Street, London W1R 2HD.

Shops and Kiosks

At properties where admission is charged there is a kiosk selling a small range of souvenirs, postcards and handbooks. At properties marked 🖰 there is a shop offering a specially selected range of gifts and publications.

Disabled Access

At properties marked ♿ a reasonable amount of what there is to see may be enjoyed by visitors in wheelchairs. If access is limited to part of the site only, details are given after the symbol. Toilets suitable for the disabled are listed where they are available.

Dogs

At properties marked ⊗ no dogs are allowed. Where the symbol ☻ is shown, dogs are allowed but must be kept on a lead. Dogs are only allowed in certain areas at properties where the symbol ☻ is shown. There are no restrictions on guide dogs or hearing dogs.

Smoking

This is not permitted in English Heritage houses.

English ⊞ Heritage

Eating out at historic properties

W hat better way to round off your visit to an English Heritage property than by relaxing in one of our restaurants, tea rooms or cafeterias. You can enjoy a range of hot food, snacks and drinks in atmospheric surroundings, often set within the historic fabric of the building itself.

You might find yourself in the original kitchens at Kenwood, one of Hurst Castle's casemates, the housekeeper's room at Audley End, or even the stable block of Boscobel House.

Look for the special symbol ⫾ in this Guide.

SPECIAL EVENTS

EACH YEAR special events of all kinds are held at many English Heritage properties all over the country. Free to English Heritage members, these include demonstrations of everyday life in medieval times, precision archery displays, battle re-enactments and performances of medieval music. For a free diary of events being held at English Heritage properties, please write to English Heritage Special Events Unit, Keysign House, 429 Oxford Street, London W1R 2HD or telephone 071-973 3457/9.

SUMMER CONCERTS

DURING THE SUMMER, you can sit back, relax and listen to music on a summer evening — classical open air concerts performed by world famous orchestras, often accompanied by fireworks displays. There is an extensive programme of concerts taking place this year at Kenwood and Marble Hill in London and also at Audley End House, Essex. For details about the concerts please write to the English Heritage Concerts Unit, Keysign House, 429 Oxford Street, London W1R 2HD or telephone 071-973 3427.

English ⌗ Heritage

The war that changed the face of Britain

THE CIVIL WAR

1642-1651
350th
ANNIVERSARY

This year sees the 350th anniversary of the beginning of the Great Civil War. Why not mark the occasion with a visit to some of the English Heritage sites connected with the Civil War? They're all marked in this Guide with the special symbol ⚔.

And, as our contribution to the anniversary celebrations, we've organised an exciting series of special events up and down the country. Thrill to the re-creation of a Civil War battle or mingle with Cavaliers and Roundheads at one of our Living History displays.

For full details of all our Civil War Events look in your 1992 Events Diary, or phone 071-973 3459.

✠ USEFUL ADDRESSES

IF YOU HAVE any general queries about information in this book, please contact the Marketing Division Head Office at English Heritage, Keysign House, 429 Oxford Street, London W1R 2HD. Tel: 071-973 3000.

Opening times for particular monuments may be checked either by telephoning the property itself where the number is given in this book, or by contacting the relevant Area Office at the address below. Some of these addresses and telephone numbers are likely to change during 1992; please look for details of changes in *English Heritage Magazine*. Refer to the map on page 13 for the relevant Area Office.

NORTH
Bessie Surtees House
41-44 Sandhill
Newcastle upon Tyne NE1 3JF
Tel. 091-261 1585

MIDLANDS (North)
Finchfield House
Castlecroft Road
Wolverhampton WV3 8BY
Tel. (0902) 765105

MIDLANDS (South)
24 Brooklands Avenue
Cambridge CB2 2BU
Tel. (0223) 455532

LONDON & SOUTH EAST
Spur 17
Government Buildings
Hawkenbury
Tunbridge Wells
Kent TN2 5AQ
Tel. (0892) 548166

LONDON HISTORIC HOUSES
The Iveagh Bequest, Kenwood
Hampstead Lane
London NW3 7JR
Tel. 081-348 1286

SOUTH WEST
Bridge House
Clifton
Bristol BS8 4XA
Tel. (0272) 734472

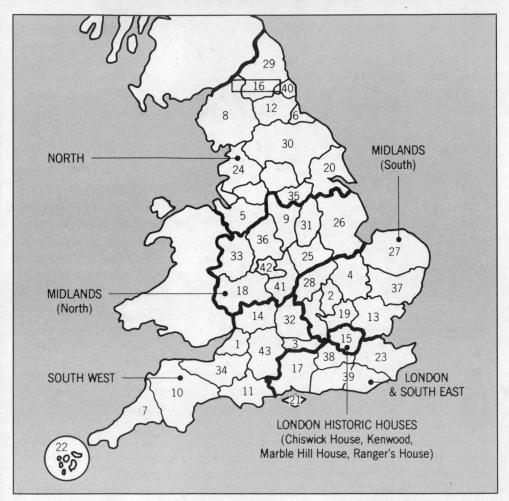

NORTH

MIDLANDS
(South)

MIDLANDS
(North)

SOUTH WEST

LONDON
& SOUTH EAST

LONDON HISTORIC HOUSES
(Chiswick House, Kenwood,
Marble Hill House, Ranger's House)

1 Avon	16 Hadrian's Wall	31 Nottinghamshire
2 Bedfordshire	17 Hampshire	32 Oxfordshire
3 Berkshire	18 Hereford & Worcester	33 Shropshire
4 Cambridgeshire	19 Hertfordshire	34 Somerset
5 Cheshire	20 Humberside	35 South Yorkshire
6 Cleveland	21 Isle of Wight	36 Staffordshire
7 Cornwall	22 Isles of Scilly	37 Suffolk
8 Cumbria	23 Kent	38 Surrey
9 Derbyshire	24 Lancashire	39 Sussex (East and West)
10 Devon	25 Leicestershire	40 Tyne and Wear
11 Dorset	26 Lincolnshire	41 Warwickshire
12 Durham	27 Norfolk	42 West Midlands
13 Essex	28 Northamptonshire	43 Wiltshire
14 Gloucestershire	29 Northumberland	
15 Greater London	30 North Yorkshire	

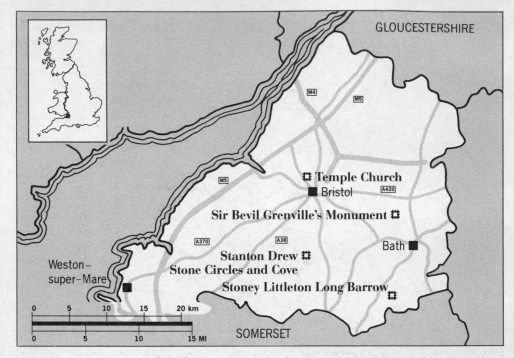

GLOUCESTERSHIRE

M4 · M5 · M5 · A420

‡ Temple Church
■ Bristol

Sir Bevil Grenville's Monument ‡

A370 · A38

Stanton Drew ‡
Stone Circles and Cove

Bath ■

Weston-super-Mare ■

Stoney Littleton Long Barrow ‡

| 0 | 5 | 10 | 15 | 20 km |

| 0 | 5 | 10 | 15 MI |

SOMERSET

A VON'S LANDSCAPE of narrow winding lanes and little villages provides a picturesque backdrop to an enormous variety of attractions. Towns include Georgian Bath, and the popular seaside resort of Weston-Super-Mare.

The county also has a rich industrial heritage. Brunel's achievements stand out, including as they do the breathtaking suspension bridge at Clifton, plus many engineering works for the Great Western Railway.

But the heart of Avon is Bristol. For centuries a great trading port, it has been the point of departure for many adventurers, a landing place for exotic goods, and a focus of industrial innovation. It still possesses a vitality and energy which many cities of greater size and wealth would find hard to match.

BRISTOL: TEMPLE CHURCH ⛪

The handsome tower and walls of this 15th century church defied the bombs of World War II. The graveyard is now a pleasant public garden.

🕐 *Exterior viewing at any reasonable time. Access to interior during shop hours (key from local florist).*

♿ 🚫

➤ *In Temple St off Victoria St (OS Map 172; ref ST 593727).* Bus: *From surrounding areas (Tel: 0272 297979).* Station: *Bristol Temple Meads ¼m.*

⚐ SIR BEVIL GRENVILLE'S MONUMENT, LANSDOWN

Commemorates the heroism of a Royalist commander and his Cornish pikemen at the Battle of Lansdown.

⏲ *Any reasonable time.*

⚐

➲ *4m NW of Bath, on N edge of Lansdown Hill, near road to Wick (OS Map 172; ref ST 721703). Bus: Badgerline 2 BR Bath Spa-Ensleigh, thence 2½m (Tel: 0225 464446). Station: Bath Spa 4½m.*

STANTON DREW CIRCLES AND COVE ⚐

A fascinating assembly of three stone circles, two avenues and a burial chamber makes this one of the finest Neolithic religious sites in the country.

⏲ *Any reasonable time but closed Sun. NB access via private land; the owner may levy a charge on all visitors to the Stone Circles.*

⚐

➲ *Circles: E of Stanton Drew village; Cove: In garden of the Druid's Arms (OS Map 172; Circles ref ST 601634, Cove ref ST 598633). Bus: Badgerline 376, 677 Bristol-Yeovil (passes BR Bristol Temple Meads), alight Pensford, 1½m (Tel: 0272 297979). Station: Bristol Temple Meads 7m.*

STONEY LITTLETON LONG BARROW ⚐

This Neolithic burial mound is about 100 feet long and has chambers where human remains once lay.

⏲ *Any reasonable time (exterior only).*

⚐

➲ *1m S of Wellow off A367 (OS Map 172; ref ST 735573). Station: Bath Spa 6m.*

English ✚ Heritage

Covenant your subscription

If you are a UK taxpayer, here's a simple way to increase the value of your subscription to English Heritage by 33% without having to pay a penny more yourself.

Taking out a Deed of Covenant means English Heritage can reclaim the income tax you have already paid. On a single adult membership subscription of £15, for example, we would be able to claim an additional £5 from the Inland Revenue.

All you have to do is agree to remain a member for the next four years and then, in the presence of a witness, sign and date the covenant form you'll find on page 157.

To avoid any worries about forgetting to renew your subscription over this period, why not combine this with payment by Direct Debit? It saves us money too. You'll find a Direct Debit form, also on page 157.

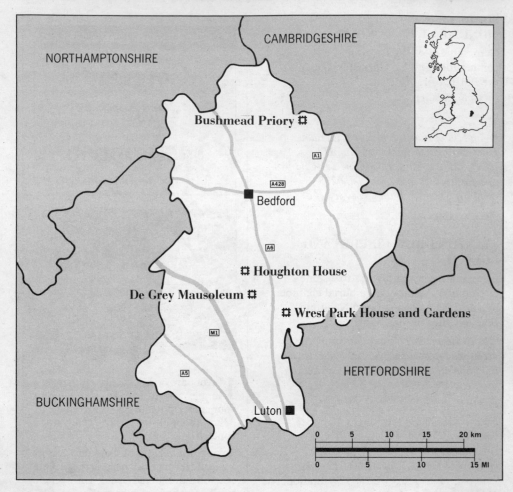

Bushmead Priory

A1

A428

Bedford

A6

Houghton House

De Grey Mausoleum

Wrest Park House and Gardens

M1

A5

HERTFORDSHIRE

BUCKINGHAMSHIRE

Luton

| 0 | 5 | 10 | 15 | 20 km |
| 0 | | 5 | 10 | 15 MI |

ONE OF THE SMALLEST counties in England, predominantly rural and scattered with villages, Bedfordshire contains some of the finest agricultural land in the country — gentle undulations, interrupted only by a dramatic escarpment of the Chilterns in the north.

Many of the villages are built of warm, golden limestone, mined from the local quarries which also supplied stone for Windsor Castle and the interior of Westminster Abbey.

The county has a rich architectural history covering most periods. It has several fine country houses, including Wrest Park House. With large attractive gardens laid out in the 18th century, later partly remodelled by 'Capability' Brown — it offers a perfect man-made setting in a naturally beautiful countryside.

BUSHMEAD PRIORY 🏛

A rare survival of the medieval refectory of an Augustinian priory, with its original timber-framed roof almost intact and containing interesting wall paintings and stained glass.

⊙ *Summer season, weekends only, Sat 10am-6pm, Sun 2pm-6pm. £1.10/85p/55p.*

P ⊗

✆ *(023062) 614*

➡ *On unclassified road near Colmworth, 2m E of B660 (OS Map 153; ref TL 115607).* Station: *St Neots 6m.*

Bushmead Priory

DE GREY MAUSOLEUM, FLITTON

A remarkable treasure-house of sculpted tombs and monuments from the 16th to 19th centuries dedicated to the de Grey family of nearby Wrest Park.

⊙ *Weekends only. Keykeeper. Access through Flitton Church.*

⊗

✆ *Area Office (0902) 765105*

➡ *Flitton, attached to church, on unclassified road 1½m W of A6 at Silsoe (OS Map 153; ref TL 059359).* Station: *Flitwick 2m.*

HOUGHTON HOUSE 🏠

Reputedly the inspiration for 'House Beautiful' in Bunyan's 'Pilgrim's Progress', the remains of this early 17th century mansion still convey elements which justify the description, including work attributed to Inigo Jones.

⊙ *Any reasonable time.*

P ♿ ⊗

➡ *1m NE of Ampthill off A418, 8m S of Bedford (OS Map 153; ref TL 039394).* Bus: *United Counties 142/3 BR Flitwick-Bedford to within ½m (Tel: 0234 262151).* Station: *Flitwick or Stewartby, both 3m.*

WREST PARK HOUSE AND GARDENS 🏠 ❀

Acres of wonderful gardens originally laid out in the early 18th century, including the Great Garden, with charming buildings and ornaments, and the delightfully intricate French Garden, with statues and fountain. The house, once the home of the de Grey family, whose Mausoleum at Flitton is nearby, was inspired by 18th century French chateaux.

⊙ *Summer season, weekends & Bank Holidays only 10am-6pm. £1.50/£1.10/75p.*

🚻 P 🍴 ⊗

✆ *(0525) 60152*

➡ *¾m E of Silsoe off A6 (OS Map 153; ref TL 093356).* Bus: *United Counties X2, X52 BR Luton-Bedford to within ½m (Tel: 0234 262151).* Station: *Flitwick 4m.*

Wrest Park: Bowling Green House, Gardens

BERKSHIRE

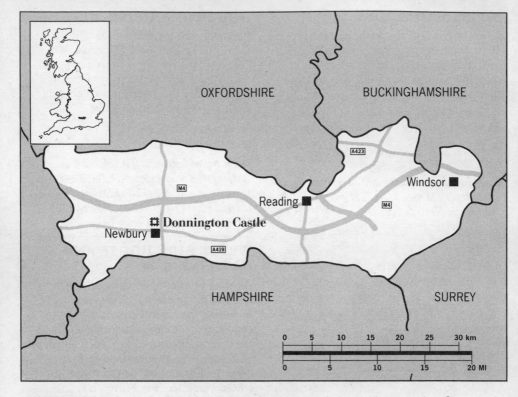

OXFORDSHIRE

BUCKINGHAMSHIRE

A423

Windsor ■

M4

Reading ■

M4

⌗ **Donnington Castle**

Newbury ■

A419

HAMPSHIRE

SURREY

```
0    5   10   15   20   25   30 km
0        5        10       15      20 MI
```

WHILE BERKSHIRE'S HISTORY extends over thousands of years, it also looks to the future, as home to Britain's own 'Silicon Valley' of high-technology companies, which cuts across the country along the M4 corridor.

During the Civil War, Berkshire divided the Royalists in Oxfordshire from the Parliamentarians in London, and was the scene of much fighting. A thousand years ago, Berkshire was part of Alfred the Great's Kingdom of Wessex. Before that, the Romans built towns here, and earlier still, traces of Iron Age man can still be seen.

While much of the history of Berkshire is now obscured, it is still possible to lose oneself in a maze of country lanes and to wander through ancient woodland.

⚔ DONNINGTON CASTLE ⛨

Built in the late 14th century, the twin towered gatehouse of this heroic castle survives amidst some impressive earthworks. The remainder was destroyed during one of the longest sieges of the Civil War, lasting nearly two years.

🕐 *All year plus Mondays in Winter.*

🅿 ♿ *(steep slopes within grounds)* ♺

➤ *1m N of Newbury off B4494 (OS Map 174; ref SU 461694). Bus: Bee Line 107, 110, 118 from Newbury (close BR Newbury). Station: Newbury 1¼m.*

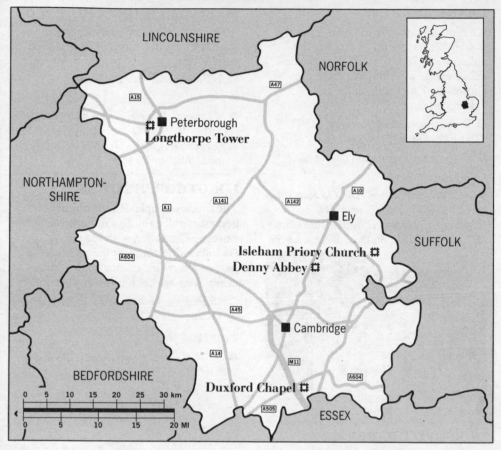

LINCOLNSHIRE

NORFOLK

A47

A15

Peterborough
Longthorpe Tower

NORTHAMPTON-
SHIRE

A1

A141

A142

A10

Ely

SUFFOLK

A604

Isleham Priory Church
Denny Abbey

A45

Cambridge

A14

M11

BEDFORDSHIRE

A604

Duxford Chapel

0 5 10 15 20 25 30 km

0 5 10 15 20 MI

A505

ESSEX

S ITTING IN THE BASIN of the Ouse, Cambridgeshire is a low-lying
county. Its northern parts are a mixture of marshland and fen, renowned
for the variety of its birdlife.

Further south, the county rises into rolling uplands, spreading itself out
into large farms. With few hedgerows, views are often panoramic.

In the heart of the Fens lies Ely, with its Norman cathedral rising
spectacularly above the surrounding countryside. Similarly, Cambridge can be
seen from miles around.

Yet the real span of Cambridgeshire history lies in the lowlands. Populated
since the Bronze Age, flooded in the Iron Age, drained in Roman times, and
flooded once more in the Middle Ages, the settlement of the Fens is as much
shaped by the battle to prevent flooding as by the forces of politics and war.

The 14th century Longthorpe Tower houses an important series of
medieval wall paintings, whilst Denny Abbey has an interesting dining hall.

19

DENNY ABBEY 🏛

What at first appears to be an attractive stone-built farmhouse is actually the remains of a 12th century Benedictine abbey which, at different times, also housed the Knights Templar and Franciscan nuns.

🕐 *Summer season, daily; Sundays only in Winter 10am-4pm. £1.10/85p/55p.*

🅿 🚫 ♿ *(grounds & ground floor only).*

✆ *(0223) 860489*

➤ *6m N of Cambridge on A10 (OS Map 154; ref TL 495684). Bus: Cambus 109 Cambridge-Ely (passes close BR Waterbeach) (Tel: 0223 423554). Station: Waterbeach 3m.*

Denny Abbey

DUXFORD CHAPEL 🏛

A medieval chapel once part of the Hospital of St John.

🕐 *Any reasonable time. Keykeeper.*

🚫

➤ *Adjacent to Whittlesford station off A505 (OS Map 154; ref TL 486472). Station: Whittlesford, adjacent.*

ISLEHAM PRIORY CHURCH 🏛

A rare example of an early Norman church which has survived little altered despite being later converted to a barn.

🕐 *Any reasonable time. Keykeeper.*

🚫

➤ *In Isleham, 16m NE of Cambridge on B1104 (OS Map 143; ref TL 642744). Bus: Cambus 122 Cambridge-Soham (Tel: 0223 423554). Station: Newmarket 8½m; Ely 9m.*

LONGTHORPE TOWER 🏛

The finest example of 14th century domestic wall paintings in northern Europe. The tower, with the Great Chamber that contains the paintings, is part of a fortified manor house. Special exhibitions are held in the upper floor.

🕐 *All year, weekends only. £1.10/85p/55p.*

🚫

✆ *(0733) 268482*

➤ *2m W of Peterborough on A47 (OS Map 142; ref TL 163983). Station: Peterborough 1½m.*

Longthorpe Tower

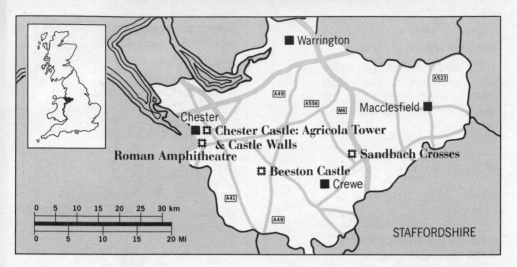

Warrington

A523

A49
A556
M6   Macclesfield ■

Chester
■✡ Chester Castle: Agricola Tower
✡ & Castle Walls
Roman Amphitheatre   ✡ Sandbach Crosses
✡ Beeston Castle
■ Crewe
A41
A49
STAFFORDSHIRE

0 5 10 15 20 25 30 km
0 5   10   15   20 MI

THE HIGH ROCKY CRAGS on which Beeston Castle sits create an imposing sight. Below lies a gentle landscape, scattered with fine churches, splendid houses, prosperous farms and large estates. From the castle itself you can gaze out over almost the entire county of Cheshire. Beyond, lie the Welsh mountains to the west and the Pennines to the east.

The county's highlight is its ancient capital of Chester. There you will find a wide range of historical periods in evidence. Roman artefacts, medieval city walls, a castle and cathedral, magnificent timber-framed Tudor houses and elegant Georgian buildings; all make it one of the most interesting cities in England to explore.

▓ BEESTON CASTLE ⌂

Standing majestically on sheer, rocky crags which fall sharply away from the castle walls, Beeston has possibly the most stunning views of the surrounding countryside of any castle in England and the rock has a history stretching back over 2,500 years.

⏰ *All year. £1.80/£1.40/90p.*

♿ ℗ 🖼 🚻 ♿

✆ *(0829) 260464*

➲ *11m SE of Chester on minor road off A49 (OS Map 117; ref SJ 537593).* Bus: *Cheshire Bus C83/5 from Chester (Tel: 0244 602666).* Station: *Chester 10m.*

Beeston Castle

21

CHESTER CASTLE: AGRICOLA TOWER AND CASTLE WALLS

Set in the angle of the city walls, this 12th century tower contains a fine vaulted chapel. There is an exhibition in the nearby Guard Room.

⊕ *All year.*

& *(parts)* ⊛

➡ *Access via Assizes Court car park on Grosvenor St. (OS Map 117; ref SJ 405658).* Bus: *From surrounding areas (Tel: 0244 602666).* Station: *Chester 1m.*

CHESTER ROMAN AMPHITHEATRE

The largest Roman amphitheatre in Britain, partially excavated. Used for entertainment and military training by the 20th Legion, based at the fortress of Deva.

⊕ *All year.*

& *(no access to amphitheatre floor)* ⊛

➡ *On Vicars Lane beyond Newgate, Chester. (OS Map 117; ref SJ 404660).* Bus: *From surrounding areas (Tel: 0244 602666).* Station: *Chester ³/₄m.*

SANDBACH CROSSES

Rare Saxon stone crosses, carved with animals, dragons and biblical scenes, in the centre of the market square. Other carved Saxon stones can be found outside the nearby church.

⊕ *Any reasonable time.*

& ⊛

➡ *Market square, Sandbach. (OS Map 118; ref SJ 758608).* Bus: *Cheshire Bus K32/3/7 from BR Sandbach (Tel: 0244 602666).* Station: *Sandbach 1½m.*

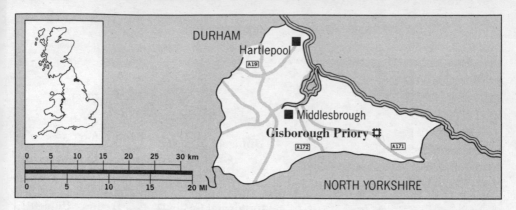

DURHAM
Hartlepool
A19
Middlesbrough
Gisborough Priory ⌗
A172   A171
NORTH YORKSHIRE

0 5 10 15 20 25 30 km
0 5 10 15 20 MI

I N 1974, the industrial conurbation on and around the Tees estuary was re-designated as the county of Cleveland. The area is an industrial powerhouse, and has long been one of the nation's industrial heartlands.

It is an area of activity which contrasts with the tranquility of Guisborough Moor, just a few miles south of Middlesbrough. Here you can find the remains of the 12th century Gisborough Priory, a welcome oasis of openness in so busy a county.

GISBOROUGH PRIORY 🏛

The impressive east end of this Augustinian priory stands like a triumphal arch in the landscape. The remains also include the gatehouse and the east end of an early 14th century church.

◷ *All year.* 75p/55p/40p.

  🚻 *(in town)* ⊕

☏ *(0287) 638301*

➲ *In Guisborough town, next to parish church. (OS Map 94; ref NZ 618163).* Bus: *Tees & District X56, 93, 256/8 from Middlesbrough (passing close BR Middlesbrough). (Tel: 0642 210131).* Station: *Marske 4½m.*

Gisborough Priory

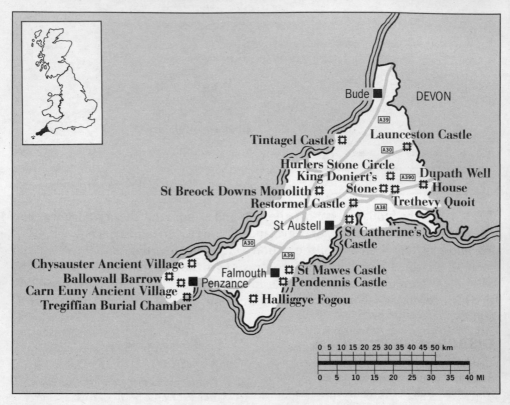

Bude

DEVON

A39

Tintagel Castle

Launceston Castle

A30

Hurlers Stone Circle

King Doniert's

Dupath Well

St Breock Downs Monolith

Stone

House

Restormel Castle

A390

A38

Trethevy Quoit

St Austell

St Catherine's Castle

A30

A39

Chysauster Ancient Village

Falmouth

St Mawes Castle

Ballowall Barrow

Penzance

Pendennis Castle

Carn Euny Ancient Village

Tregiffian Burial Chamber

Halliggye Fogou

0 5 10 15 20 25 30 35 40 45 50 km

0 5 10 15 20 25 30 35 40 MI

C ORNWALL'S CHARACTER stems from two clear roots. It has a Celtic tradition unique in England, and parallels of its history and culture can be found in places like Brittany, and Galicia in northern Spain. Its landscape too is unique: wild and rugged, with a harsh backbone of granite, and an unforgiving coastline racked by Atlantic waves.

For this reason, sheltered harbours have always been a feature of Cornwall. Many have had castles built to protect them, including Pendennis and St Mawes.

The secluded nature of many harbours, and the picturesque fishing villages climbing up behind, have been a driving force behind Cornwall's thriving tourist industry.

Hidden away you can also find more secluded remnants of ancient Cornish history. There are stone circles, fogous, burial chambers and ancient villages, like Chysauster, dating from the second century AD, but built on an even earlier Iron Age site.

Most spectacular of all is Tintagel Castle. Built on a headland and now in ruins, it catches perfectly the mystical spirit of this rugged county.

BALLOWALL BARROW, ST JUST

In a spectacular position, on a cliff's edge looking towards Land's End, this is an unusual Bronze Age chambered tomb with a complex layout.

⏲ *Any reasonable time.*

⊛

➲ *1m W of St Just, near Carn Gloose (OS Map 203; ref SW 354313). Bus: Western National 1A, 10/A/B, 11 BR Penzance-St Just, thence 1m (Tel: 0736 69469). Station: Penzance 8m.*

CARN EUNY ANCIENT VILLAGE

The remains of an Iron Age settlement, with foundations of stone huts and an intriguing curved underground passage, or fogou.

⏲ *Any reasonable time.*

🅿 ⊛

➲ *1¼m SW of Sancreed off A30 (OS Map 203; ref SW 402289). Bus: Western National 1A, 10/A/B, BR Penzance-St Just, to within 2m (Tel: 0736 69469). Station: Penzance 6m.*

CHYSAUSTER ANCIENT VILLAGE

On a windy hillside, overlooking the wild and spectacular coast, is this deserted Romano-Cornish village with a 'street' of eight well preserved houses, each comprising a number of rooms around an open court.

⏲ *Summer season. £1.20/90p/60p.*

⍾ 🅿 ⊛

📞 *(0736) 61889*

➲ *2½m NW of Gulval off B3311 (OS Map 203; ref SW 473350). Bus: Western National 16 BR Penzance-St Ives to within 1½m (Tel: 0736 69469). Station: Penzance 3½m.*

DUPATH WELL HOUSE, CALLINGTON

A charming granite-built well house set over a holy well c.1500 and still almost complete.

⏲ *All year, plus Mondays in Winter.*

⊛

➲ *1m E of Callington off A388 (OS Map 201; ref SX 374693). Bus: Western National 76 Plymouth-Callington, then 1m (Tel: 0752 664011). Station: Gunnislake 4½m.*

HALLIGGYE FOGOU

One of several strange underground tunnels, associated with Iron Age villages, which are unique to Cornwall. This one is perhaps the finest and most mysterious.

⏲ *Summer season.*

A torch is advisable. ⊛

➲ *5m SE of Helston off B3293 E of Garras on Trelowarren estate (OS Map 203; ref SW 714239). Bus: Truronian 311 from Helston (Tel: 0872 73453); Western National 2/A links Helston with BR Penzance (Tel: 0736 69469). Station: Penryn 10m.*

Chysauster Ancient Village

HURLERS STONE CIRCLE ⚑

Within a host of prehistoric remains on Bodmin Moor, these three Bronze Age stone circles in a line are some of the best examples of ceremonial standing stones in the South-West.

🕐 *Any reasonable time.*

🅿 *(lay-by)* ✆

➤ *½m NW of Minions off B3254 (OS Map 201; ref SX 258714). Bus: Deeble 234 BR Liskeard-Higher Tremar, thence 1½m (Tel: 0579 62226). Station: Liskeard 7m.*

KING DONIERT'S STONE, ST CLEER

Two decorated pieces of a 9th century cross with an inscription believed to commemorate Durngarth, King of Cornwall, who drowned c.875.

🕐 *Any reasonable time.*

✆

➤ *1m NW of St Cleer off B3254 (OS Map 201; ref SX 236688). Bus: Deeble 234 BR Liskeard-St Cleer, thence ½m (Tel: 0579 62226). Station: Liskeard 4m.*

LAUNCESTON CASTLE ⚔

Set on the motte of the original Norman castle and commanding the town and surrounding countryside, the shell keep and tower survive of this medieval castle which controlled the main route into Cornwall.

🕐 *All year. £1.10/85p/55p.*

♿ *(outer bailey)* ✆ ▦

☎ *(0566) 772365*

➤ *In Launceston (OS Map 201; ref SX 330846). Bus: Western National 76 Plymouth-Launceston (Tel: 0752 664011).*

🏰 PENDENNIS CASTLE ⚔

This castle is a testament to the quality of the coastal defences erected by Henry VIII. The well preserved granite gun fort and outer ramparts with great angled bastions defended against invasion from the sea, but it was captured from the land after a long siege during the Civil War.

🕐 *All year. £1.80/£1.40/90p.*

🚻 🅿 🍴 ♿ *(grounds, part keep)*

✆ ⫣*(summer season only)* ◻ ▤ ◻ ▦

☎ *(0326) 316594*

➤ *On Pendennis Head 1m SE of Falmouth (OS Map 204; ref SW 824318). Station: Falmouth Docks ½m.*

Pendennis Castle

Launceston Castle

RESTORMEL CASTLE ⌂

Perched on a high mound, surrounded by a deep moat, the huge circular keep of this splendid Norman castle survives in remarkably good condition.

⏲ *Summer season. £1.10/85p/55p.*

⚥ P ⊗ ⌖

✆ *(0208) 872687*

➲ *1½m N of Lostwithiel off A390 (OS Map 200; ref SX 104614). Station: Lostwithiel 1½m.*

Restormel Castle

ST BREOCK DOWNS MONOLITH ⌂

A prehistoric standing stone, originally about 16 feet high, set in beautiful countryside.

⏲ *Any reasonable time.*

⊛

➲ *On St Breock Downs, 3¾m SSW of Wadebridge off A39 (OS Map 200; ref SW 968683). Station: Roche 5½m.*

ST CATHERINE'S CASTLE, FOWEY ⌂

A small fort built by Henry VIII to defend Fowey harbour, with fine views of the coastline and river estuary.

⏲ *Any reasonable time.*

⊛

➲ *¾m SW of Fowey off A3082 (OS Map 200; ref SX 118508). Bus: Western National 24 St Austell-Fowey, thence ¾m (Tel: 0872 40404). Station: Par 4m.*

ST MAWES CASTLE ⌂ ✤

Together with Pendennis, St Mawes Castle, also built by Henry VIII, guarded the entrance to safe anchorage in the Carrick Roads. Its three huge circular bastions with gun ports were formidable defences indeed but today stand in delightful sub-tropical gardens.

⏲ *All year. £1.20/90p/60p.*

⚥ P ⊗ ♿ *(grounds & ground floor only)* ⌖ ⌖ ⌖

✆ *(0326) 270526*

➲ *In St Mawes on A3078 (OS Map 204; ref SW 842328). Ferry: St Mawes Ferry Co from Falmouth, Prince of Wales Pier (Tel: 0209 861020). Station: Penmere, via Prince of Wales Pier, 4½m by sea.*

St Mawes Castle

TINTAGEL CASTLE

The spectacular setting for this legendary castle of King Arthur is the wild and windswept Cornish coast. Clinging precariously to the edge of the cliff face are the extensive ruins of a medieval royal castle built by Richard, Earl of Cornwall, younger brother of Henry III. Despite extensive excavation since the 1930's and a mass of picturesque legend, Tintagel is still an enigma, its history full of gaps and the nature of its earlier occupation quite uncertain.

All year. £1.80/£1.40/90p.

P *(in Tintagel village)*

(0840) 770328

On Tintagel Head, ½ mile along track from Tintagel, no vehicles, (OS Map 200; ref SX 048891). Bus: *Fry's Bus Service from Wadebridge (Tel: 0840 770256).*

Tintagel Castle

TREGIFFIAN BURIAL CHAMBER, ST BURYAN

A Neolithic or early Bronze Age chambered tomb by the side of a country road.

Any reasonable time.

2m SE of St Buryan on B3315 (OS Map 203; ref SW 430245). Station: *Penzance 5½m.*

TRETHEVY QUOIT, ST CLEER

An ancient Neolithic burial chamber, possibly over 4,000 years old, standing nine feet high and consisting of five standing stones surmounted by a huge capstone.

Any reasonable time.

1m NE of St Cleer off B3254 (OS Map 201; ref SX 259688). Bus: *Deeble 234 BR Liskeard-Tremar (Tel: 0579 62226).* Station: *Liskeard 3½m.*

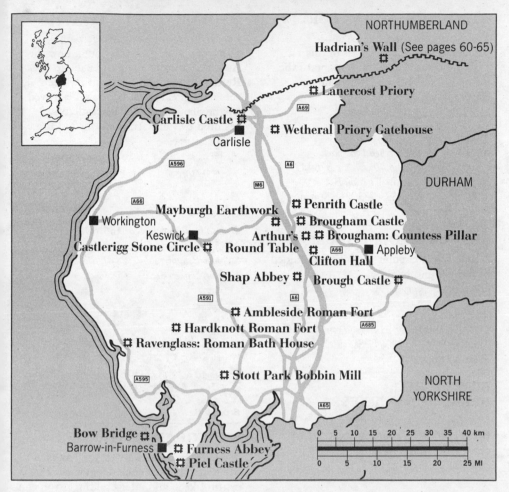

NORTHUMBERLAND

Hadrian's Wall (See pages 60-65)

⚓ Lanercost Priory

A69

Carlisle Castle ⚓
Carlisle

⚓ Wetheral Priory Gatehouse

A596

A6

DURHAM

M6

A66

Mayburgh Earthwork

⚓ Penrith Castle

■ Workington

⚓ ⚓ Brougham Castle

Keswick ■

Arthur's ⚓ ⚓ Brougham: Countess Pillar

Castlerigg Stone Circle ⚓

Round Table ⚓ A66 ■ Appleby

Clifton Hall

Shap Abbey ⚓

Brough Castle ⚓

A591

A6

⚓ Ambleside Roman Fort

⚓ Hardknott Roman Fort

A685

⚓ Ravenglass: Roman Bath House

⚓ Stott Park Bobbin Mill

NORTH
YORKSHIRE

A595

0 5 10 15 20 25 30 35 40 km

A65

0   5   10   15   20   25 MI

Bow Bridge ⚓
Barrow-in-Furness ■ ⚓ Furness Abbey
⚓ Piel Castle

CUMBRIA IS A LAND of steep-sided mountains falling into deep black lakes, rolling isolated fells and desolate moorland. The Lake District includes well-known peaks like Helvellyn, The Old Man of Coniston, and Scafell — the highest in England.

Cumbria has been inhabited since prehistoric times. There is a Neolithic stone circle at Castlerigg. During the Roman era a road was driven from Brougham, through Ambleside, across Hardknott Pass, and on to Ravenglass. Remains of Roman forts can still be seen at Hardknott and Ambleside. At both Brougham and Brough there are impressive 13th century castles, and Ravenglass has the remains of a Roman bath house.

A more recent historical monument is Stott Park Bobbin Mill, built 150 years ago, and still in working order.

AMBLESIDE ROMAN FORT ⚔

In a field at the head of Lake Windermere lie the remains of this 1st and 2nd century fort, built to guard the Roman road between Brougham and Ravenglass.

⊙ *Any reasonable time. (NT)*

☻

➥ *200yds W of Waterhead car park, Ambleside. (OS Map 90; ref NY 376033). Bus: CMS 518, 555, W1 from BR Windermere (Tel: 0539 733221). Station: Windermere 5m.*

ARTHUR'S ROUND TABLE ⛫

A prehistoric circular earthwork bounded by a ditch and bank.

⊙ *Any reasonable time.*

♿ ☻

➥ *At Eamont Bridge, 1m S of Penrith. (OS Map 90; ref NY 523284). Station: Penrith 1½m.*

BOW BRIDGE, BARROW-IN-FURNESS

Late medieval stone bridge across Mill Beck, carrying a route connected with nearby Furness Abbey.

⊙ *Any reasonable time.*

☻

➥ *½m N of Barrow-in-Furness, on minor road off A590 near Furness Abbey (OS Map 96; ref SD 224715). Bus: CMS 6 Barrow-in-Furness — Dalton, to within ¾m (Tel: 0229 821325). Station: Barrow-in-Furness 1½m.*

BROUGH CASTLE ⛫

Perched on a superb vantage point overlooking an old trade route, now the A66, this ancient site dates back to Roman times. The 12th century keep replaces an earlier stronghold destroyed by the Scots in 1174. The castle was restored by Lady Anne Clifford in the 17th century.

⊙ *All year (closed Mon & Tue in Winter). 75p/55p/40p.*

☻

✆ *(0228) 31777*

➥ *8m SE of Appleby S of A66. (OS Map 91; ref NY 791141). Bus: Grand Prix BR Kirkby Stephen-Brough (Tel: 0228 812812). Station: Kirkby Stephen 6m.*

Brough Castle

⚐ BROUGHAM CASTLE ⛫

These impressive ruins on the banks of the River Eamont include an early 13th century keep and later buildings. You can climb to the top of the keep and survey the domain of its eccentric one-time owner Lady Anne Clifford, who restored the castle in the 17th century. There is a small exhibition of Roman tombstones from the nearby fort.

⊙ *All year (closed Mon & Tue in Winter). £1.10/85p/55p.*

🅿 ♿ *(excluding keep)* ☻

✆ *(0768) 62488*

➥ *1½m SE of Penrith. (OS Map 90; ref NY 537290). Station: Penrith 2m.*

BROUGHAM: COUNTESS PILLAR

An unusual monument, bearing sundials and family crests, erected in 1656 by Lady Anne Clifford to commemorate her parting with her mother in 1616.

⏲ *Any reasonable time.*

☻

➡ *1m SE of Brougham on A66. (OS Map 90; ref NY 546289).* Station: *Penrith 2½m.*

CASTLERIGG STONE CIRCLE ⋔

Possibly one of the earliest Neolithic stone circles in Britain, its 33 stones stand in a beautiful setting.

⏲ *Any reasonable time. (NT)*

☻

➡ *1½m E of Keswick. (OS Map 90; ref NY 293236).* Bus: *CMS 104 BR Penrith-Keswick, to within ½m (Tel: 0228 48484).* Station: *Penrith 16m.*

Brougham Castle

⋈ CARLISLE CASTLE ⋈

This impressive medieval castle, where Mary Queen of Scots was once imprisoned, has a long and tortuous history of warfare and family feuds. A portcullis hangs menacingly over the gatehouse passage, there is a maze of passages and chambers, endless staircases to lofty towers and you can walk the high ramparts for stunning views. There is also a medieval manor house in miniature: a suite of medieval rooms furnished as they might have been when used by the castle's former constable. The castle is the home of the Museum of the King's Own Border Regiment.

⏲ *All year, plus Mondays in Winter. (Opens 9.30am daily). £1.80/£1.40/90p*

♦♦ ℗ *(disabled only)* ♿ *(except interiors of buildings)* ☐ ⊗ ⓜ

✆ *(0228) 31777*

➡ *N of Carlisle town centre. (OS Map 85; ref NY 397563).* Bus: *From surrounding areas (Tel: 0228 48484).* Station: *Carlisle ½m.*

Carlisle Castle

CLIFTON HALL

The surviving tower block of a 15th century manor near the site of the last battle fought on English soil, between Bonnie Prince Charlie's Highlanders and the Duke of Cumberland's Dragoons.

⏲ *All year.*

🐕

➤ *In Clifton next to Clifton Hall Farm, 2m S of Penrith on A6. (OS Map 90; ref NY 530271). Station: Penrith 2½m.*

FURNESS ABBEY

Set in a beautiful valley are extensive red sandstone ruins of the wealthy abbey founded in 1123 by Stephen, later King of England. This abbey first belonged to the Order of Savigny and later to the Cistercians.

⏲ *All year. £1.80/£1.40/90p.*

🚻 🅿 🎧 ♿ 📷 🐕 📋

☎ *(0229) 823420*

➤ *1½m N of Barrow-in-Furness, on minor road off A590. (OS Map 96; ref SD 218717). Bus: CMS 6 Barrow-in-Furness — Dalton, to within ½m (Tel: 0229 821325). Station: Barrow-in-Furness 2m.*

Furness Abbey

HADRIAN'S WALL

See pages 60-65.

HARDKNOTT ROMAN FORT

One of the most dramatic Roman sites in Britain, with stunning views across the Lakeland fells. This fort, built between AD120 and 138, controlled the pass on the road from Ravenglass to Ambleside. There are visible remains of granaries, the headquarters building and the commandant's house, with a bath house and parade ground outside the fort.

⏲ *Any reasonable time. Access may be hazardous in Winter.*

🅿 🐕

➤ *9m NE of Ravenglass, at W end of Hardknott Pass. (OS Map 96; ref NY 218015). Station: Eskdale (Dalegarth) (Ravenglass & Eskdale Rly) 3m.*

LANERCOST PRIORY

This Augustinian priory was founded c.1166. The nave of the church, which is intact and in use as the local parish church, contrasts with the ruined chancel, transepts and priory buildings.

⏲ *Summer season. 75p/55p/40p.*

🅿 ♿ 📷 🐕

☎ *(06977) 3030*

➤ *Off minor road S of Lanercost, 2m NE of Brampton. (OS Map 86; ref NY 556637). Bus: CMS/Northumbria 685 Carlisle — Newcastle-upon-Tyne to within 1½m (Tel: 0228 48484). Station: Brampton 3m.*

MAYBURGH EARTHWORK 🏛

An impressive prehistoric circular earthwork, with banks up to 15 feet high which enclose a central area of one and a half acres containing a single large stone.

🕐 *Any reasonable time.*

🖐

➡ *At Eamont Bridge, 1m S of Penrith off A6. (OS Map 90; ref NY 519285). Station: Penrith 1½m.*

◀ PENRITH CASTLE 🏰

This 14th century castle, set in a park on the edge of the town, was built to defend Penrith against repeated attacks by Scottish raiders.

🕐 *Park opening hours.*

👫 🖐

➡ *Opposite Penrith railway station. (OS Map 90; ref NY 513299). Station: Penrith, adjacent.*

Lanercost Priory

PIEL CASTLE 🏰

The ruins of a 14th century castle of the abbots of Furness, accessible by boat from Roa Island. There are remains of the massive keep and inner and outer baileys, defended by curtain walls and towers.

🕐 *Any reasonable time. Access by ferry from Roa Island: Summer weekdays from 11am subject to tides. Winter by arrangement, tel (0229) 820983 weekdays, (0229) 821741 weekends.*

🖐

➡ *On Piel Island, 3¼m SE of Barrow. (OS Map 96; ref SD 233636). Bus: CMS 12 Barrow-in-Furness — Roa Island (Tel: 0229 821325). Station: Barrow-in-Furness 4m to Roa Island.*

RAVENGLASS: ROMAN BATH HOUSE 🦅

Whilst little can be seen of the Roman fort which stood nearby, the walls of the bath house which served it are among the most complete Roman remains in Britain.

🕐 *Any reasonable time.*

🖐

➡ *¼m E of Ravenglass, off minor road leading to A595. (OS Map 96; ref NY 088961). Station: Ravenglass, adjacent.*

SHAP ABBEY 🏛

The striking tower and other remains of this Premonstratensian abbey, founded in the 12th century, stand in a remote and isolated location.

🕐 *Any reasonable time.*

🅿 ♿ 🖐

➡ *1½m W of Shap on bank of River Lowther. (OS Map 90; ref NY 548153). Bus: CMS 107 Penrith-Kendal, to within 1½m (Tel: 0228 48484) Station: Penrith 10m.*

STOTT PARK BOBBIN MILL

When this working mill was built in 1835 it was typical of the many mills in the Lake District which grew up to supply the spinning and weaving industry in Lancashire but have since disappeared. A remarkable opportunity to see a demonstration of the machinery and techniques of the Industrial Revolution.

⊙ *Open: Summer season (closes at dusk if before 6pm). £1.80/1.40/90p.*

⫟ 🅿 ♿ *(ground floor only)* 🛈 ⊗

✆ *(04395) 31087*

➲ *½m N of Finsthwaite near Newby Bridge. (OS Map 96; ref SD 373883). Bus: CMS 518 Ulverston-Grasmere to within 1½m (Tel: 0539 733221). Station: Grange-over-Sands 8m.*

Stott Park Bobbin Mill

WETHERAL PRIORY GATEHOUSE

The gatehouse of a Benedictine priory was preserved at the Dissolution by serving as the vicarage for the parish church.

⊙ *All year.*

⊗

➲ *On minor road in Wetheral village, 6m E of Carlisle on B6263. (OS Map 86; ref NY 468542). Bus: CMS 73-5 Carlisle-Wetherall (Tel: 0228 48484). Station: Carlisle 5m.*

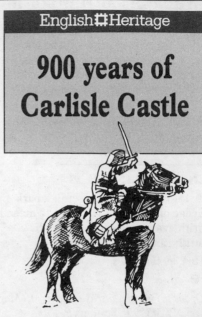

English ⌗ Heritage

900 years of Carlisle Castle

E xactly 900 years ago the Normans put the seal on their conquest of the North with the construction of Carlisle Castle.

To mark this anniversary, you can see a fascinating display of Norman weaponry and tactics, as well as two mounted knights, on August 22 and 23. There will also be a chance to experience everyday medieval life on May 3 and 4.

These, as well as all our other events, are free to English Heritage members. You'll find full details in your 1992 Events Diary or phone 071-973 3459.

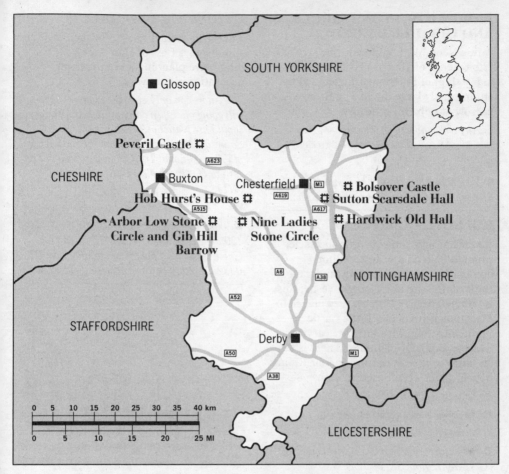

A COUNTY OF CONTRASTS, Derbyshire's historic monuments range from Neolithic stone circles to medieval castles and 18th century houses.

Three English country houses, each representing a different century's interpretation of the form, can be seen within a few miles of each other: Hardwick Old Hall, Bolsover Castle, and Sutton Scarsdale Hall, each only a short distance from the M1.

The Derbyshire countryside presents similar contrasts. To the north and west, the Peak District National Park contains huge tracts of wild, desolate moorland criss-crossed by white drystone walls — with deep wooded valleys containing delightfully unspoilt villages. At the heart of the Park, set among the romantic peaks and dales is the pretty village of Castleton; itself at the foot of Peveril Castle with its spectacular views of the entire Peak District.

35

ARBOR LOW STONE CIRCLE AND GIB HILL BARROW ⋒

A fine Neolithic monument, this 'Stonehenge of Derbyshire' comprises many slabs of limestone, surrounded by an unusually large ditch. The Bronze Age barrow at Gib Hill is nearby.

⊘ *Any reasonable time.(The farmer who owns the right of way to the site may levy a charge.)*

⊛

➲ *½m W of A515 2m S of Monyash (OS Map 119; ref SK161636).* Station: *Buxton 10m.*

⚒ BOLSOVER CASTLE ⋒

An enchanting and romantic spectacle, situated high on a wooded hilltop dominating the surrounding landscape. Built on the site of a Norman castle, this is largely an early 17th century mansion. Most delightful is the 'Little Castle', a bewitching folly with intricate carvings, frescoes and wall-paintings. There is also an impressive 17th century Indoor Riding School which is still used on occasions.

⊘ *All year. £1.80/£1.40/90p.*

⫟ 🅿 ♿ *(grounds only)* ⊛ 🖴

☏ *(0246) 823349*

➲ *In Bolsover, 6m E of Chesterfield on A632 (OS Map 120; ref SK 471707).* Bus: *E Midland 81, Chesterfield Transport 81-3, 281/ 2 Chesterfield-Bolsover (pass close BR Chesterfield) (Tel: 0332 292200).* Station: *Chesterfield 6m.*

HARDWICK OLD HALL ⋒

This large ruined house, finished in 1591, still displays Bess of Hardwick's innovative planning and interesting decorative plasterwork.

⊘ *Visitors can only view the exterior as work is still going on. Open daily until dusk. Visitors should use National Trust car park, Easter Saturday-31 October 10.30am-6pm. Entry fee of £1 to National Trust grounds refundable on visit to Hardwick New Hall and Garden. (NT)*

⊛

➲ *9½m SE of Chesterfield, off A6175 (OS Map 120; ref SK 463638).* Bus: *E Midland 63 Chesterfield-Nottingham to within 1¾m (Tel: 0332 292200).* Station: *Chesterfield 9½m.*

Bolsover Castle

HOB HURST'S HOUSE ⋒

A square prehistoric burial mound with an earthwork ditch and outer bank.

⊘ *Any reasonable time.*

⊛

➲ *From unclassified road off B5057, 9m W of Chesterfield (OS Map 119; ref SK 287692).* Bus: *East Midland X66, Hulleys X67, 170 from Chesterfield, to within 2m (Tel: 0332 292200).* Station: *Chesterfield 9m.*

NINE LADIES STONE CIRCLE, STANTON MOOR

Once part of the burial site for 300-400 people, this moorland Early Bronze Age circle is 50 feet across.

⏱ *Any reasonable time.*

⊛

➲ *From unclassified road off A6, 5m SE of Bakewell (OS Map 119; ref SK 253635). Bus: Hulleys 170 Matlock-Bakewell (passes close BR Matlock), to within 1m (Tel: 0332 292200). Station: Matlock 4½m.*

PEVERIL CASTLE

There are breathtaking views of the Peak District from this castle, perched high above the pretty village of Castleton. The great square tower stands almost to its full height.

⏱ *All year. £1.10/85p/55p.*

⊛

☎ *(0433) 20613*

➲ *On S side of Castleton, 15m W of Sheffield on A625 (OS Map 110; ref SK 150827). Bus: SYT/Hulleys 272/4 BR Sheffield-Castleton (Tel: 0332 292200). Station: Hope 2½m.*

Peveril Castle

SUTTON SCARSDALE HALL

The dramatic shell of a great early 18th century baroque mansion.

⏱ *Any reasonable time (exterior only).*

🅿 ♿ ⊛

➲ *Between Chesterfield and Bolsover, 1½m S of Arkwright Town (OS Map 120; ref SK 441690). Bus: E Midland 48 Chesterfield-Bolsover (Tel: 0332 292200). Station: Chesterfield 5m.*

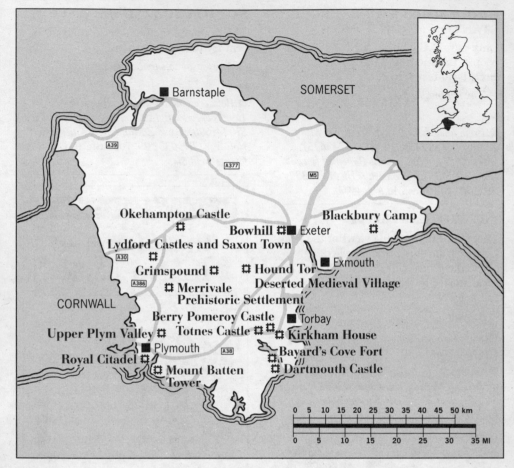

Barnstaple

SOMERSET

A39

A377

M5

Okehampton Castle

Blackbury Camp

Bowhill Exeter

Lydford Castles and Saxon Town

A30

Grimspound

Hound Tor

Exmouth

Deserted Medieval Village

Merrivale

CORNWALL

Prehistoric Settlement

A386

Berry Pomeroy Castle

Torbay

Upper Plym Valley

Totnes Castle

Kirkham House

Plymouth

A38

Bayard's Cove Fort

Royal Citadel

Mount Batten
Tower

Dartmouth Castle

| 0 | 5 | 10 | 15 | 20 | 25 | 30 | 35 | 40 | 45 | 50 km |

| 0 | 5 | 10 | 15 | 20 | 25 | 30 | 35 MI |

N O SINGLE IMAGE can capture the essence of Devon. The boggy moorland of Dartmoor contrasts with the genteel towns of the coastal areas. The northern coastline is rugged and bracing, while the southern coastline enjoys some of the mildest weather in the country.

Dartmoor once supported many farming communities. Evidence of Bronze Age settlements can be found at Grimspound and Merrivale, and a deserted medieval village can be seen at Hound Tor.

Nearer the coast, the rivers open out into beautiful estuaries. At the mouth of the Dart lies the once busy port of Dartmouth. Protected by a series of forts, its castle still stands — one of the earliest designed for artillery.

A great port which still retains its status is Plymouth, marking the western edge of Devon's southern coastline. Since the time of the Spanish Armada it has been the base of the Royal Navy, with a proud seafaring tradition.

BERRY POMEROY CASTLE 🏰

A romantic late medieval castle, dramatically sited half-way up a wooded hillside, looking out over a deep ravine and stream. It is unusual in combining the remains of a large castle with a flamboyant courtier's mansion.

🕐 *Summer season. £1.50/£1.10/75p.*

🅿 ♦ ♿ *(grounds & ground floor only)* ⊗

📞 *(0803) 866618*

➡ *2½m E of Totnes off A385 (OS Map 202; ref SX 839623). Station: Totnes 3½m.*

Berry Pomeroy Castle

BLACKBURY CAMP 🏛

This Iron Age hill fort, defended by a bank and ditch and now covered by trees and foliage, was occupied up until c.AD100.

🕐 *Any reasonable time.*

⊗

➡ *1½m SW of Southleigh off B3174/A3052 (OS Map 192; ref SY 188924). Station: Honiton 6½m.*

BOWHILL 🏤

A mansion of considerable status built c.1500 by a member of the Holland family who were wealthy local landowners. The impressive Great Hall is being carefully restored by English Heritage craftsmen using traditional materials and techniques and is now open to the public whilst this work continues.

🕐 *Summer season, weekdays 10am-3.30pm, closed Bank Holidays and following Tuesdays.*

⊗

📞 *Area Office (0272) 734472.*

➡ *1½m SW of Exeter on B3212. (OS Map 192; ref SX 906916). Bus: Exeter Mini-Bus C, P from City Centre (Tel: 0392 56231). Station: Exeter, St. Thomas ¾m.*

DARTMOOR: GRIMSPOUND 🏛

One of the most famous prehistoric sites of Dartmoor, this late Bronze Age settlement displays the remains of 24 huts in an area of four acres enclosed by a stone wall.

🕐 *Any reasonable time.*

⊗

➡ *6m SW of Moretonhampstead off B3212 (OS Map 191; ref SX 701809).*

DARTMOOR: HOUND TOR DESERTED MEDIEVAL VILLAGE

The remains of the dwellings, stables and grain stores of three or four medieval farmsteads, first occupied in the Bronze Age. They lie in a starkly beautiful moorland setting.

🕐 *Any reasonable time.*

⊗

➡ *1½m S of Manaton off Ashburton road. Park in Hound Tor car park, ½m walk (OS Map 191; ref SX 746788).*

DARTMOUTH CASTLE

This brilliantly positioned defensive castle juts out into the narrow entrance to the Dart estuary, with the sea lapping at its foot. It was one of the first castles constructed with artillery in mind and has seen 450 years of fortification and preparation for war.

☉ *All year. £1.50/£1.10/75p.*

⫟ P *(limited)* ⎕ ⊗

✆ *(0803) 833588*

➥ *1m SE of Dartmouth off B3205, narrow approach road, (OS Map 202; ref SX 887503). Bus: Devon General 22 Brixham-Kingswear (with connections from BR Paignton), thence vehicle ferry to Dartmouth and local ferry to Castle. (Tel: 0803 613226). Station: Paignton 8m via vehicle ferry.*

Dartmouth Castle

DARTMOUTH: BAYARD'S COVE FORT

Set among the picturesque gabled houses of Dartmouth, on the waterfront at the end of the quay, this is a small artillery fort built 1509-10 to defend the harbour entrance.

☉ *Any reasonable time.*

⊗

➥ *In Dartmouth, on riverfront (OS Map 202; ref SX 879510). Bus: Devon General 22 Brixham-Kingswear (with connections from BR Paignton), thence vehicle ferry to Dartmouth (Tel: 0803 613226). Station: Paignton 7m via vehicle ferry.*

DARTMOOR: MERRIVALE PREHISTORIC SETTLEMENT

Two long rows of standing stones stretching up to 864 feet across the moors, together with the remains of an early Bronze Age village.

☉ *Any reasonable time.*

⊗

➥ *1m E of Merrivale (OS Map 191; ref SX 553746). Station: Gunnislake 10m.*

KIRKHAM HOUSE, PAIGNTON

A well preserved medieval stone house, much restored and repaired, which gives a fascinating insight into life in a town residence in the 15th century.

☉ *Exterior viewing only, at any reasonable time.*

⊗

➥ *In Kirkham St, off Cecil Rd, Paignton (OS Map 202; ref SX 885610). Bus: From surrounding areas (Tel: 0803 613226). Station: Paignton ½m.*

LYDFORD CASTLES AND SAXON TOWN ⌂

Standing above the lovely gorge of the River Lyd, this 12th century tower was notorious as a prison. The earthworks of the original Norman fort are to the south. A Saxon town once stood nearby and its layout is still discernible.

🕐 *Any reasonable time.*

🐕

➲ *In Lydford off A386 8m S of Okehampton (OS Map 191; Castle ref SX 510848, Fort ref SX 509847). Bus: Down's 118 from Tavistock with connections from Plymouth (Tel: 0392 382800).*

MOUNT BATTEN TOWER ⌂

A 17th century gun tower, 30 feet high and with original windows and vaulted roof. There are good views across Plymouth Sound from here.

🕐 *1st Thur in month 2-4pm, by prior written permission of the Officer Commanding, RAF Mount Batten, Plymouth.*

🐕

➲ *In Plymstock, on Mount Batten Point (OS Map 201; ref SX 488533). Bus: Western National 7 from Plymouth (Tel: 0752 664011). Station: Plymouth 5m.*

Kirkham House, Paignton

OKEHAMPTON CASTLE ⌂

The ruins of the largest castle in Devon stand above a river surrounded by splendid woodland. There is still plenty to see, including the Norman motte and the jagged remains of the keep. There is a picnic area and lovely woodland walks.

🕐 *All year. £1.50/£1.10/75p.*

🚻 🅿 ♿ 🍴 *(picnic tables available)* 🎧

☎ *(0837) 52844*

➲ *1m SW of Okehampton off A30 (OS Map 191; ref SX 584942). Bus: Devon General 51, Bow Belle 628, Jennings 629 from Exeter (some pass BR Exeter St David's) to within 1m (Tel: 0392 382800).*

Okehampton Castle

ROYAL CITADEL, PLYMOUTH ▮

A large, dramatic 17th century fortress, with walls up to 70 feet high, built to defend the coastline from the Dutch and still in use today.

⊙ *By guided tour only (1½ hours) at 12pm and 2pm, 18 July-30 September. For security reasons tours may be suspended at short notice. Please telephone (0752) 660582 or Plymouth Tourist Information Centre for details of where to assemble. £1.50/£1/75p. Exterior viewing at any reasonable time.*

⊗

✆ *(0752) 660582*

➡ *At E end of Plymouth Hoe (OS Map 201; ref SX 480538). Bus: From surrounding areas (Tel: 0752 664011). Station: Plymouth 1¼m.*

TOTNES CASTLE ▮

By the North Gate of the hill town of Totnes you will find a superb motte and bailey castle, with splendid views across the roof tops and down to the River Dart. It is a symbol of lordly feudal life and a fine example of Norman fortification.

⊙ *All year. £1.20/90p/60p.*

🅿 *(70yds, small charge)* ⊗ 🛍

✆ *(0803) 864406*

➡ *In Totnes, on hill overlooking the town (OS Map 202; ref SX 800605). Station: Totnes ¼m.*

Totnes Castle

UPPER PLYM VALLEY, DARTMOOR ⏷

Scores of prehistoric and medieval sites covering six square miles of ancient landscape. Huts, stone walls, burial mounds and standing stones reflect human settlement and industrial activity in the area from Neolithic times to the 20th century.

⊙ *Any reasonable time.*

⊗

➡ *4m E of Yelverton (OS Map 202).*

English ✠ Heritage

Conservation in action at Bowhill

The Great Hall of the 15th century mansion of Bowhill near Exeter is now open to the public for the first time. Come along and see how English Heritage craftsmen have used traditional materials and methods to restore this historic building.
See page 39 for directions and opening times.

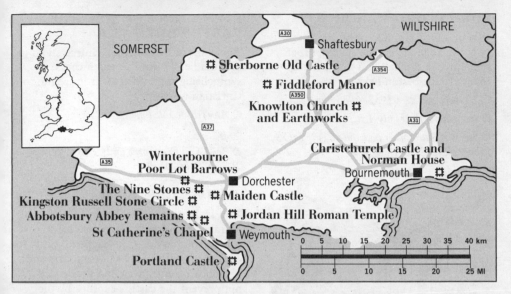

T HOMAS HARDY WROTE about a rural Dorset facing up to the upheavals of the 19th century. Yet much of the rustic charm he described still survives. The county market town of Dorchester retains many of the aspects — and buildings — he described. It is an excellent point from which to explore Dorset.

Most of the county's coastline has something interesting about it, with strange formations like Durdle Door and Lulworth Cove. All along the coast there are fossils embedded in the rocks and along the cliffs. Chesil Beach, a long, narrow shingle and pebble spit, extends for about ten miles, before finally reaching the Isle of Portland, and Portland Castle.

Alternatively, you could head north from Dorchester, where you will find the ruins of 12th century Sherborne Old Castle, and villages with peculiar names like Piddletrenthide or Minterne Magna.

ABBOTSBURY ABBEY REMAINS ⚓

In a delightful village of stone and thatch cottages are the remains of a cloister building of this Benedictine abbey, founded in 1044.

🕐 Any reasonable time.

🅿 Ⓢ

➲ In Abbotsbury, off B3157, near churchyard (OS Map 194; ref SY 578852). Station: Upwey 7½m.

CHRISTCHURCH CASTLE AND NORMAN HOUSE 🏰 🏛

Early 12th century Norman keep, and Constable's house, built c.1160.

🕐 Any reasonable time.

Ⓢ

➲ In Christchurch, near the Priory (OS Map 195; ref SZ 160927). Bus: From surrounding areas (Tel: 0202 673555). Station: Christchurch ¾m.

FIDDLEFORD MANOR 🏠

Part of a medieval manor house, with a remarkable interior. The splendid roof structures in the hall and upper living room are the best in Dorset.

🕐 *Keykeeper. Tel. (0305) 860853 for details.*

🅿 ♿ *(ground floor only-1 step)* ⊗

➡ *1m E of Sturminster Newton off A357 (OS Map 194; ref ST 801136).*

Fiddleford Manor

JORDAN HILL ROMAN TEMPLE, WEYMOUTH 🜚

Foundations of a Romano-Celtic temple enclosing an area about 240 feet square.

🕐 *Any reasonable time.*

⊗

➡ *2m NE of Weymouth off A353 (OS Map 194; ref SY 698821). Bus: Southern National A from Weymouth (Tel: 0305 783645). Station: Upwey or Weymouth, both 2m.*

KINGSTON RUSSELL STONE CIRCLE 🏛

A Bronze Age stone circle of 18 stones, at the convergence of five public footpaths.

🕐 *Any reasonable time.*

⊗

➡ *2m N of Abbotsbury (OS Map 194; ref SY 577878). Station: Dorchester West or South, both 8m.*

KNOWLTON CHURCH AND EARTHWORKS 🏠 🏛

The ruins of this Norman church stand in the middle of Neolithic earthworks, symbolising the transition from pagan to Christian worship.

🕐 *Any reasonable time.*

♿ ⊗

➡ *3m SW of Cranborne on B3078 (OS Map 195; ref SU 024100).*

MAIDEN CASTLE 🏛

This is the finest Iron Age hill fort in Britain, set amongst some delightful rolling countryside. The earthworks are enormous, with a series of ramparts and complicated entrances, but they could not prevent the castle's capture by the Romans c.AD43.

🕐 *Any reasonable time.*

🅿 ⊗

➡ *2½m SW of Dorchester off B3147 on town side of ringroad (OS Map 194; ref SY 670885). Station: Dorchester South or West, both 2m.*

THE NINE STONES, WINTERBOURNE ABBAS 🏛

Remains of a prehistoric stone circle consisting of nine standing stones.

🕐 *Any reasonable time.*

⊗

➡ *1½m W of Winterbourne Abbas, S of A35 (OS Map 194; ref SY 611904). Bus: Southern National 31, X31 Weymouth-Taunton (pass BR Dorchester South and Axminster) (Tel: 0305 783645). Station: Dorchester West or South, both 5m.*

⚑ PORTLAND CASTLE ⛫

One of the best preserved of Henry VIII's coastal forts, built of white Portland stone. Now standing quietly overlooking the harbour, it was originally intended to thwart attack by the Spanish and French, and changed hands several times during the Civil War.

🕐 *Summer season. £1.10/85p/55p.*

🅿 ⊗ ♿ *(exterior & ground floor only-1 deep step)*

☎ *(0305) 820539*

➡ *Overlooking Portland harbour adjacent to RN helicopter base (OS Map 194; ref SY 684743). Bus: Southern National 1, 10, 501, Smith's Coaches Weymouth-Portland (Tel: 0305 783645). Station: Weymouth 4½m.*

Portland Castle

ST CATHERINE'S CHAPEL, ABBOTSBURY ⛪

A small stone chapel, set on a hilltop, with an unusual roof and small turret used as a lighthouse.

🕐 *All year plus Mondays in Winter.*

⊗

➡ *½m S of Abbotsbury by pedestrian track from village off B3157 (OS Map 194; ref SY 572848). Station: Upwey 7½m.*

⚑ SHERBORNE OLD CASTLE ⛫

The ruins of this early 12th century castle are a testament to the 16 days it took Cromwell to capture it during the Civil War, after which it was abandoned.

🕐 *All year. £1.10/85p/55p.*

🅿 ⊗ ♿

☎ *(093581) 2730*

➡ *½m E of Sherborne on N side of lake (OS Map 183; ref ST 647167). Station: Sherborne ¾m.*

Sherborne Old Castle

WINTERBOURNE POOR LOT BARROWS ⛨

An important Bronze Age cemetery consisting of 44 barrows of different shapes and sizes.

🕐 *Any reasonable time.*

⊗

➡ *2m W of Winterbourne Abbas, S of junction of A35 with minor road to Compton Valence (OS Map 194; ref SY 590906). Bus: Southern National 31, X31 Weymouth-Taunton (pass BR Dorchester South and Axminster) (Tel: 0305 783645). Station: Dorchester West or South, both 7m.*

DURHAM

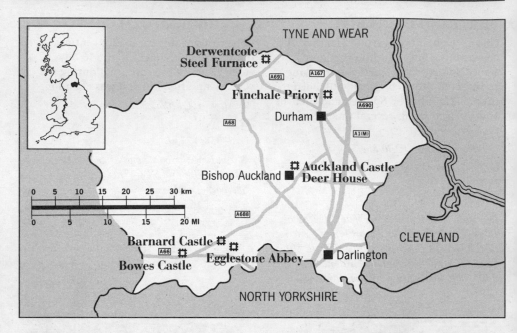

D URHAM HAS BOTH a medieval heritage and beautiful countryside to offer. The city of Durham is the centre of the county, and for many centuries was the seat of the Prince Bishops, rulers of the area in all but name. The magnificent architecture of the city reflects their power and grandeur. Near to the city are the extensive ruins of the 13th century Benedictine Finchale Priory.

The county's rugged yet breathtaking scenery is epitomised by Teesdale in the west. Here, on the bank of the Tees, you will find the noble ruins of Barnard Castle. Nearby is Bowes Castle, also built in the 12th century, and the picturesque remains of Egglestone Abbey.

AUCKLAND CASTLE DEER HOUSE, BISHOP AUCKLAND 🏛

A charming building erected in 1760 in the park of the Bishops of Durham so that the deer could shelter and find food.

⏰ *Park opening hours.*

🚫

➲ *In Bishop Auckland Park, just N of town centre on A689. (OS Map 93; ref NZ 216305).* Bus: *From surrounding areas (Tel: 091-386 4411).* Station: *Bishop Auckland 1m.*

BOWES CASTLE 🏰

Massive ruins of Henry II's tower keep, three storeys high and set within the earthworks of a Roman fort.

⏰ *Any reasonable time.*

🚫

➲ *¼m W of Bowes on A66, 4m W of Barnard Castle. (OS Map 92; ref NY 992135).*

BARNARD CASTLE

The substantial remains of this large
castle stand on a rugged escarpment
overlooking the River Tees. You can still
see parts of the 14th century Great Hall
and the cylindrical 12th century tower,
built by the Baliol family.

⏱ *All year. £1.10/85p/55p.*

♿ 🍴 👬 *(in town)* 🅿

✆ *(0833) 38212*

➲ *In Barnard Castle (OS Map 92; ref NZ
049165).* Bus: *United 75/A, X75 BR
Darlington-Barnard Castle (Tel: 0325
468771).*

DERWENTCOTE STEEL FURNACE

The Derwent Valley steel works were
once the centre of the British steel
industry, and Derwentcote, built in the
18th century, is the earliest and most
complete authentic steel making furnace
to have survived. Closed during the
1870's and allowed to fall into disrepair,
the furnace has now been restored and
opened to the public by English Heritage
and includes a small exhibition.

⏱ *Summer season £1.10/85p/55p.*

🅿 🅿

✆ *(0207) 562573*

➲ *10m SW of Newcastle on A694 between
Rowland's Gill and Hamsterley. (OS Map 88;
ref NZ 131566).* Bus: *Go-Ahead Northern
745 Newcastle-upon-Tyne — Consett (Tel:
091-386 4411)* Station: *Blaydon 7m.*

Derwentcote Steel Furnace

Barnard Castle

EGGLESTONE ABBEY

Picturesque remains of a 12th century
abbey, located in a bend of the River
Tees. Substantial parts of the church and
abbey buildings remain.

⏱ *Any reasonable time.*

🅿 ♿ 🍴 🅿

➲ *1m S of Barnard Castle on minor road off
B6277. (OS Map 92; ref NZ 062151).* Bus:
*United 75/A, X75 BR Darlington-Barnard
Castle, thence 1m (Tel: 0325 468771).*

FINCHALE PRIORY

These beautiful 13th century priory
remains are located beside the curving
River Wear.

⏱ *Any reasonable time.*

🅿 🅿

➲ *3m NE of Durham, on minor road off A167.
(OS Map 88; ref NZ 297471).* Bus:
*Gardiners 737 Durham — Chester-le-Street
(passes close BR Durham) (Tel: 0388 814417).*
Station: *Durham 5m.*

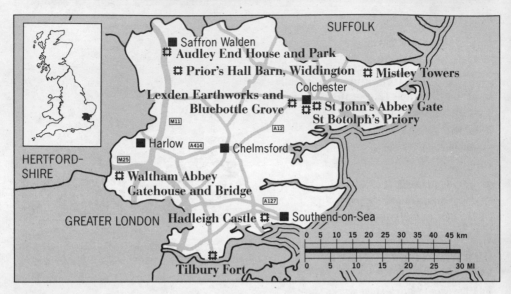

E SSEX IS A COUNTY of extremes. Its southern area forms part of central London, which gradually runs out into small, scattered rural communities in the north such as Finchingfield and Thaxted.

Because the southern part of Essex forms an edge to London's sprawling fringes, the county is often seen as urban, whereas it is in fact largely agricultural, and steeped in history.

The county's historic importance stems from the decision by the Romans to make Colchester their capital. Evidence of Roman occupation can still be seen, as well as the remains of buildings from later periods, including the Middle Ages.

AUDLEY END HOUSE AND PARK 🏛 ✳

A palatial Jacobean country mansion set in magnificent parklands landscaped by 'Capability' Brown. Thirty rooms are on view, including reception rooms by Robert Adam, with a fascinating collection of paintings and period furniture. The Great Hall has a massive, exquisitely carved screen, elegant double staircase and panelled ceiling. The early Victorian garden on the east front has recently been restored to its former splendour.

🕐 *Summer season, Tues-Sun and Bank Holidays, 1-6pm; park and gardens open at 12 noon. Last admissions one hour before closing. £4.50/£3.40/£2.30.*

🚻 🍴 🅿 ♿ *(substantial ground-floor area & gardens only)* ⊗ 🖶 ⬚ ⬚ 📷

📞 *(0799) 522399*

➡ *1m W of Saffron Walden on B1383 (M11 exits 8, 9 Northbound only, & 10) (OS Map 154; ref TL 525382). Station: Audley End 1¼m.*

COLCHESTER: LEXDEN EARTHWORKS AND BLUEBOTTLE GROVE

Parts of a series of earthworks, once encompassing 12 square miles, which protected Iron Age Colchester and were subsequently added to by the conquering Romans.

⌚ *Any reasonable time.*

⊗

➡ *2m W of Colchester off A604 (OS Map 168; ref TL 963240).* Bus: *Colchester Transport 9/A from Town Centre (passing BR St Botolph's) (Tel: 0206 44449).* Station: *Colchester or Colchester Town, both 2½m.*

COLCHESTER: ST BOTOLPH'S PRIORY 🏛

The nave, with an impressive arcaded west end, of the first Augustinian priory in England.

⌚ *Any reasonable time.*

⊗

➡ *Colchester, near St Botolph's station (OS Map 168; ref TL 999249).* Bus: *From surrounding areas (Tel: 0206 571451).* Station: *Colchester Town, adjacent.*

Audley End House

COLCHESTER: ST JOHN'S ABBEY GATE 🏛

This fine abbey gatehouse, in East Anglian flintwork, survives from the Benedictine abbey of St John.

⌚ *Any reasonable time (exterior only).*

⊗ ♿

➡ *On S side of central Colchester (OS Map 168; ref TL 998248).* Bus: *From surrounding areas (Tel: 0206 571451).* Station: *Colchester Town ¼m.*

HADLEIGH CASTLE 🏰

From the curtain wall and two towers, which survive almost to their full height, the land drops steeply away, giving splendid views of the Essex marshes and Thames estuary.

⌚ *Any reasonable time.*

⊗ ♿ *(hilly).*

☎ *(0702) 555632*

➡ *¾m S of A13 at Hadleigh (OS Map 178; ref TQ 810860).* Bus: *Thamesway and Southend Transport services from surrounding areas to within ½m (Tel: 0702 558421 or 355711).* Station: *Leigh-on-Sea 1½m by footpath.*

MISTLEY TOWERS 🏛

The remains of one of only two churches designed by the great architect Robert Adam. Built in 1776, it is unusual in having towers at both the east and west ends.

⌚ *All year plus Mondays in Winter. Keykeeper.*

⊗ ♿ *(exterior only).*

➡ *On B1352, 1½m E of A137 at Lawford, 9m E of Colchester (OS Map 169; ref TM 116320).* Bus: *Eastern National 102-4 Colchester-Harwich (Tel: 0206 571451).* Station: *Mistley ¼m.*

PRIOR'S HALL BARN, WIDDINGTON

One of the finest surviving medieval barns in south-east England and representative of the group of aisled barns centred on north-west Essex.

⏱ *Any reasonable time.*

⊗ ⚿

➲ *In Widdington, on unclassified road 2m SE of Newport, off B1383, (OS Map 167; ref TL 538319). Bus: Eastern National 301 Bishops Stortford-Saffron Walden (Tel: 0279 652476). Station: Newport 2m.*

TILBURY FORT ⊞

The best and largest example of 17th century military engineering in England, commanding the Thames and showing the development of fortifications over the following 200 years. Exhibitions, the powder magazine and the bunker-like 'casemates' demonstrate how the fort protected London from seaborne attack.

⏱ *All year. £1.80/£1.40/90p.*

⊗ 🗎 ⚶ ⌒ ⚿ *(exterior, fort square & magazines).*

✆ *(0375) 858489*

➲ *½m E of Tilbury off A126 (OS Map 177; ref TQ 651754). Bus: Priory Minicoaches 380 BR Standford-le-Hope — Tilbury Riverside (Tel: 0268 541062). Station: Tilbury Riverside ½m. Station liable to close in 1992. Alternative: Tilbury Town 1½m.*

Tilbury Fort

Prior's Hall Barn, Widdington

WALTHAM ABBEY GATEHOUSE AND BRIDGE ⚷

The late 14th century abbey gatehouse, part of the north range of the cloister and the medieval 'Harold's Bridge' of one of the great monastic foundations of the Middle Ages.

⏱ *Any reasonable time.*

⊛

➲ *In Waltham Abbey off A112 (OS Map 166; ref TL 381008). Bus: Frequent services by different operators from BR Waltham Cross (Tel: 0992 556765). Station: Waltham Cross 1¼m.*

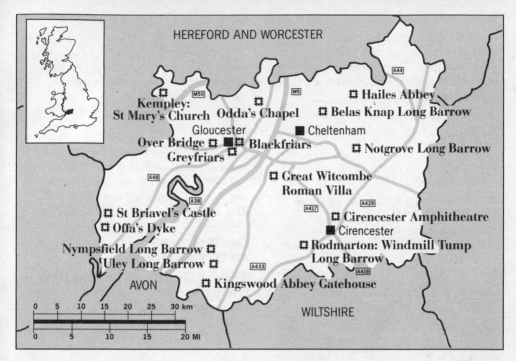

S TRETCHING ACROSS GLOUCESTERSHIRE are the beautiful Cotswold Hills. Revealing an endless series of enchanting views, scattered with golden-yellow cottages, the Cotswolds in sunshine belie their winter harshness.

This picture of Gloucestershire is famous, and draws many tourists during the summer. But there is also a largely undiscovered heritage of prehistoric remains, Roman ruins and medieval buildings.

There is a Neolithic long barrow at Belas Knap, and another at Hetty Pegler's Tump, near Stroud. Close to Cirencester is a 2nd century Roman amphitheatre, and 13th century Hailes Abbey lies near Winchcombe.

But most hidden away, in a remote western corner in the Forest of Dean, lie Offa's Dyke and the 12th century St Briavel's Castle.

BELAS KNAP LONG BARROW 🏛

A good example of a Neolithic long barrow, with the mound still intact and surrounded by a stone wall. The chamber tombs, where the remains of 31 people were found, have been opened up so visitors can see inside.

🕐 *Any reasonable time.*

🚫

➡ *2m S of Winchcombe, near Charlton Abbots (OS Map 163; ref SP 021254). Bus: Castleways from Cheltenham to within 1¾m (Tel: 0242 602949). Station: Cheltenham 9m.*

BLACKFRIARS, GLOUCESTER ⚓

A small Dominican priory church converted into a rich merchant's house at the Dissolution. Most of the original 13th century church remains, including a rare scissor-braced roof.

⊙ *Summer season weekdays only 10am-3.15pm; closed Bank Holidays and following Tuesdays.*

⊗

✆ *Area Office (0272) 734472*

➡ *In Ladybellegate St off Southgate St and Blackfriars Walk (OS Map 162; ref SO 830186). Bus: From surrounding areas (Tel: 0452 425543). Station: Gloucester ½m.*

Blackfriars, Gloucester

CIRENCESTER AMPHITHEATRE ⚶

The grass covered banks of this large well preserved Roman amphitheatre, which once held stone terraces and wooden seating for 8,000 spectators, still rise to 25 feet above the arena floor.

⊙ *Any reasonable time.*

⊛

➡ *Next to bypass W of town — park in town or on Cotswold Ave to S of amphitheatre by obelisk (OS Map 163; ref SP 020014). Bus: Alex Cars/Anton rail-link from BR Kemble (Tel: 0452 425543). Station: Kemble 4m.*

GREAT WITCOMBE ROMAN VILLA ⚶

The remains of a large villa, overlooking an enchanting valley. Built around three sides of a courtyard, it had a luxurious bath-house complex.

⊙ *Any reasonable time.*

🅿 ⊛

➡ *5m SE of Gloucester, off A417, ½m S of reservoir in Witcombe Park (OS Map 163; ref SO 899144). Bus: Cheltenham & District 50 BR Gloucester-Cheltenham to within 1½m (Tel: 0452 27516). Station: Gloucester 6m.*

GREYFRIARS, GLOUCESTER ⚓

The remains of a late 15th/early 16th century Franciscan friary church which has undergone many changes over the years.

⊙ *Any reasonable time.*

♿ ⊛

➡ *On Greyfriars Walk, behind Eastgate Market off Southgate St (OS Map 162; ref SO 830186). Bus: From surrounding areas (Tel: 0452 425543). Station: Gloucester ½m.*

HAILES ABBEY ⚓

Set in attractive wooded pastureland, the remains of the cloisters and foundations, with examples of high quality sculpture in the site museum, show us the extent of the wealth of this 13th century Cistercian abbey.

⊙ *All year. £1.60/£1.20/80p. (NT)*

⚥ 🅿 🎧 ♿ *(general access, 1 step to museum)* Ⓜ ⊛

✆ *(0242) 602398*

➡ *2m NE of Winchcombe off B4632 (OS Map 150; ref SP 050300). Bus: Castleways from Cheltenham to within 1½m (Tel: 0242 602949). Station: Cheltenham 10m.*

KINGSWOOD ABBEY GATEHOUSE ⛪

The 16th century gatehouse, with a richly carved mullioned window, is all that remains of this Cistercian abbey which prospered in the Middle Ages due to the wool trade.

🕐 *Any reasonable time (exterior). Key for interior obtained from shop nearby.*

🚻 *(adjacent to monument)* ⊗

➥ *In Kingswood off B4060 1m SW of Wotton-under-Edge (OS Map 162; ref ST 748919). Bus: Badgerline 309 Bristol-Dursley (Tel: 0272 297979). Station: Yate 8m.*

NOTGROVE LONG BARROW ⚑

A Neolithic burial mound with chambers for human remains opening from a stone-built central passage.

🕐 *Any reasonable time.*

🅿 ⊗

➥ *1½m NW of Notgrove off B4068 (OS Map 163; ref SP 096211). Bus: Pulham's Moreton-in-Marsh — Cheltenham pass close BR Moreton-in-Marsh (Tel: 0451 20369).*

Hailes Abbey

NYMPSFIELD LONG BARROW ⚑

Overlooking the River Severn to the Forest of Dean, with a picnic site nearby, this chambered Neolithic long barrow is 90 feet long.

🕐 *Any reasonable time.*

🅿 ⊗ 🚻 *(public; 150yds)*

➥ *1m NW of Nympsfield on B4066 (OS Map 162; ref SO 795014). Bus: Stroud Valleys 15, 39 Stroud-Dursley (pass close BR Stroud) (Tel: 0453 763421). Station: Stroud 5m.*

ODDA'S CHAPEL, DEERHURST ⛪

A rare Anglo-Saxon chapel attached, rather oddly, to a half-timbered farmhouse. It lay undiscovered for many years and has been partly rebuilt and restored.

🕐 *All year plus Mondays in Winter.*

⊗

➥ *In Deerhurst (off B4213) at Abbots Court SW of parish church (OS Map 150; ref SO 869298). Bus: Swanbrook Coaches BR Gloucester-Tewkesbury (Tel: 0452 425543). Station: Cheltenham 8m.*

OFFA'S DYKE

Part of the great earthwork built by Offa, King of Mercia 757-96, from the Severn estuary to the Welsh coast as a defensive boundary to his kingdom. This section is in lovely walking country and is part of the Offa's Dyke long-distance footpath.

🕐 *Any reasonable time.*

⊗

➥ *½m SE of Tintern (access suitable only for those wearing proper walking shoes; not suitable for the young, old or infirm) (OS Map 162; ref SO 545005). Bus: Red & White 69 Chepstow-Monmouth to within ½m (Tel: 0633 265100). Station: Chepstow 7m.*

OVER BRIDGE 🏛

A pioneering single-arch masonry bridge spanning the River Severn, built by Thomas Telford 1825-27.

🕐 *Any reasonable time.*

🚫

➡ *1m NW of Gloucester city centre at junction of A40 (Ross) & A419 (Ledbury) (OS Map 162; ref SO 817196). Bus: Frequent services by different operators from BR Gloucester (Tel: 0452 425543). Station: Gloucester 2m.*

ST BRIAVEL'S CASTLE 🏰

This splendid 12th century castle is now used as a youth hostel which seems appropriate for a building set in such marvellous walking country. There is also a fine Norman church nearby.

🕐 *Any reasonable time (exterior). Bailey open summer season, daily 1pm-4pm.*

🚫

➡ *7m NNE of Chepstow off B4228 (OS Map 162; ref SO 559046). Station: Chepstow 8m.*

ST MARY'S CHURCH, KEMPLEY 🏛

A delightful Norman church with superb wall paintings from the 12th-14th centuries which were only discovered beneath white-wash in 1871.

🕐 *All year plus Mondays in Winter.*

🚫

➡ *1m N of Kempley off B4024, 6m NE of Ross-on-Wye (OS Map 149; ref SO 649313). Station: Ledbury 8m.*

ULEY LONG BARROW (HETTY PEGLER'S TUMP) 🏛

Named after the wife of its 17th century owner, but dating from around 3000BC, this 180 foot long Neolithic chambered burial mound is unusual in that its mound is still intact.

🕐 *Any reasonable time.*

🚫

➡ *3½m NE of Dursley on B4066 (OS Map 162; ref SO 790000). Bus: Stroud Valleys 15, 39 Stroud-Dursley (pass close BR Stroud) Tel: 0453 763421). Station: Stroud 6m.*

WINDMILL TUMP LONG BARROW, RODMARTON 🏛

A chambered Neolithic long barrow estimated to contain 5,000 tons of stone.

🕐 *Any reasonable time.*

🚫

➡ *1m SW of Rodmarton off A433 6m SW of Cirencester (OS Map 163; ref ST 933973). Bus: Alex Cars from BR Kemble (Tel: 0452 425543). Station: Kemble 5m.*

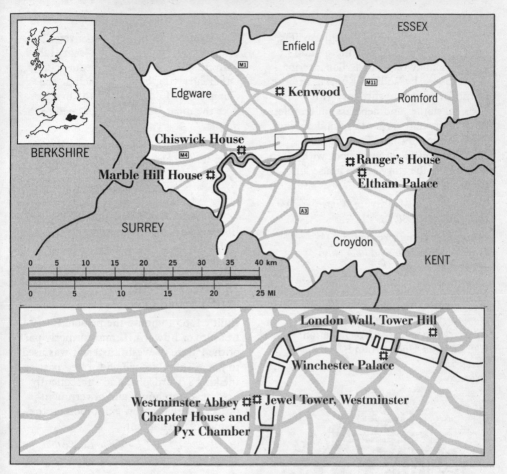

BUSTLING, NOISY, VIBRANT and exciting — London is all these, yet so much more. Its unique heritage of cultural and historic attractions has beckoned visitors and travellers alike for hundreds of years.

There are so many obvious places to see when you visit London that it is easy to by-pass less well-known but no less interesting attractions.

Some nestle close to famous landmarks. While thousands of visitors marvel at Westminster Abbey each year, many miss the Chapter House next to it, which contains some of the finest examples of medieval English sculpture.

Further up the Thames is Chiswick, with its fine Palladian villa, Chiswick House. Nearby is Marble Hill House in Twickenham, which is home to an important collection of paintings and Georgian furniture.

Near Hampstead, to the north, lies Kenwood, containing one of England's finest private collections of paintings.

55

CHISWICK HOUSE ⌂ ※

One of the first English Palladian villas, built c.1725 for Lord Burlington and internationally renowned. The interior decoration is by William Kent, as are the beautiful Italianate gardens, with classical statues and neoclassical temples. Both house and gardens are undergoing extensive restoration. There is an exhibition on the ground floor with a film telling the story of the house and gardens.

🕐 *All year, plus Mondays in Winter, 26 Dec & 1 Jan. £2/£1.50/£1.*

🚻 *(in grds)* 🅿 *(off west-bound A4)*
🎧 ♿ *(exterior & ground floor only)*
🖨 ⊙ 🛈

✆ *081-995 0508*

➲ *Burlington Lane, W4.* Bus: *LT 190, 290 Hammersmith-Richmond; E3 Greenford-Chiswick (Tel: 071-222 1234).* Station: *Chiswick ½m.* Underground: *Turnham Green 1m.*

Chiswick House

ELTHAM PALACE ⌂

The most delightful feature of this 13th century royal palace is the Great Hall with its splendid hammer-beam roof. Other surviving buildings include the Chancellor's Lodgings and the bridge over the moat, which are not open to the public.

🕐 *Summer season, Sun & Thur only 10am-6pm; Winter, Sun & Thur only 10am-4pm.*

⊗

✆ *081-854 2242*

➲ *¾m N of A20 off Court Yard, SE9.* Bus: *Frequent from surrounding areas (Tel: 071-222 1234).* Station: *Eltham or Mottingham, both ½m.*

JEWEL TOWER, WESTMINSTER ⌂

Built c.1365 to house the personal treasure of Edward III and formerly part of the Palace of Westminster. It was used to house valuables which formed part of the king's 'wardrobe', and subsequently used as a storehouse and government office. There is a new exhibition on the history of Parliament.

🕐 *All year. £1.80/£1.40/90p. Liable to be closed at short notice.*

⊗

✆ *071-222 2219*

➲ *Opposite S end of Houses of Parliament (Victoria Tower).* Bus: *Frequent from surrounding areas (Tel: 071-222 1234.)* Station: *Charing Cross ¾m, Victoria and Waterloo, both 1m.* Underground: *Westminster ¼m.*

KENWOOD, THE IVEAGH BEQUEST 🏛 ✳

Standing in splendid grounds on the edge of Hampstead Heath, Kenwood contains the most important private collection of paintings ever given to the nation. There is a selection of Old Masters, among the finest a Self Portrait by Rembrandt and paintings by British artists such as Turner, Reynolds and Gainsborough. The outstanding neoclassical house itself was remodelled by Robert Adam, 1764-73, who created the magnificent Library. Many rooms contain displays of English neoclassical furniture. Outside, the historic landscaped park, with sloping lawns and a lake, form a perfect setting to the lakeside concerts held here in the summer.

🕐 *All year, plus Mondays in Winter, 26 Dec & 1 Jan.*

🛍 ♦♦ 🅿 🍴 ⊛ ♿ *(ground floor only; ♦♦ for ♿) 🛍 ⊛*

📞 *081-348 1286*

➡ *Hampstead Lane, NW3. Bus: LT 210 BR Finsbury Park-Golders Green (Tel: 071-222 1234). Station: Hampstead Heath 1½m. Underground: Highgate 1m.*

Kenwood

The Concert Bowl at Kenwood

The English Summer just wouldn't be the same without the traditional season of English Heritage open air concerts.

There's music to suit every taste, from Bach to Bernstein and Elgar to Ellington, performed by some of England's finest orchestras.

You can enjoy an evening of open air music by the lakeside at Kenwood in Hampstead, on the banks of the Thames at Marble Hill House in Twickenham or within the delightful gardens at Audley End. The choice is yours.

This year's highlights include the Royal Opera Company, returning for their fourth visit to Kenwood on June 21 and the English National Opera performing Puccini's *La Boheme* at Marble Hill on 16 August.

And don't forget that members of English Heritage enjoy reduced rate admission to most concerts in this year's programme.

For full details please phone our concerts section on 071-973 3427.

LONDON WALL, TOWER HILL 🔥

The best preserved piece of the Roman Wall, heightened in the Middle Ages, that formed part of the eastern defences of the City of London.

⏱ *Any reasonable time.*

🚻 ♿ ⊗

➡ *Near Tower Hill underground station, EC3.* Bus: *Frequent from surrounding areas (Tel: 071-222 1234).* Station: *Fenchurch Street ¼m.* Underground: *Tower Hill, adjacent.*

MARBLE HILL HOUSE 🏛 ✳

A magnificent Thames-side Palladian villa built 1724-29 and set in 66 acres of parkland. The Great Room, recently restored, has lavish gilded decoration and architectural paintings by Panini. The house also contains an important collection of early Georgian furniture.

⏱ *All year, plus Mondays in Winter, 26 Dec & 1 Jan.*

🚻 🍴 ♿ 🅿 *(at Richmond end of Marble Hill Park)* ♿ *(exterior & ground floor only;* 🚻 *for* ♿*)* 🎧 ⊕ 🗍

✆ *081-892 5115*

➡ *Richmond Road, Twickenham.* Bus: *Frequent from surrounding areas (Tel: 071-222 1234).* Station: *St Margarets ½m.* Underground: *Richmond 1m.*

Marble Hill House

RANGER'S HOUSE 🏛

A handsome red brick villa built c.1700, on the edge of Greenwich Park, with a splendid bow-windowed gallery. It houses a remarkable series of Jacobean portraits and a collection of musical instruments.

⏱ *All year, plus Mondays in Winter, 26 Dec & 1 Jan.*

🚻 🅿 *(in Chesterfield Walk; limited)* ♿ *(lift)* ⊗ 🎧 🗍

✆ *081-853 0035*

➡ *Chesterfield Walk, Blackheath, SE10.* Bus: *LT 53 Oxford Circus-Plumstead (Tel: 071-222 1234).* Station: *Maze Hill ½m.*

Rangers House

WINCHESTER PALACE, SOUTHWARK 🏛

The west gable end, with its unusual round window, is the prominent feature of the remains of the Great Hall of this 13th century town house of the Bishops of Winchester, badly damaged by fire in 1814.

⏱ *Any reasonable time.*

🚻 ♿ ⊗

➡ *Near Southwark Cathedral, at corner of Clink St & Storey St, SE1.* Bus: *Frequent from surrounding areas (Tel: 071-222 1234).* Station & Underground: *London Bridge ¼m.*

WESTMINSTER ABBEY: CHAPTER HOUSE, PYX CHAMBER AND ABBEY MUSEUM ⚑

The Chapter House, built by the royal masons in 1250 and faithfully restored in the 19th century, contains some of the finest examples of medieval English sculpture to be seen. The building is octagonal, with a central column, and still has its original floor of glazed tiles. Its uses have varied, but in the 14th century it was used as a meeting place for the Benedictine monks of the abbey, and also for members of Parliament. The 11th century Pyx Chamber now houses the Abbey treasures, reflecting its use as the strongroom of the exchequer from the 14th to 19th centuries. The Abbey museum contains medieval royal effegies.

🕑 *All year, plus Mondays in Winter. Liable to be closed at short notice on state occasions.* £1.80/£1.40/90p.

🔊 *(50p)* ⊗ ⑦

✆ *071-222 5897*

➡ *Approach either through the Abbey or through Dean's Yard and the cloister. Bus: Frequent from surrounding areas (Tel: 071-222 1234). Station: Victoria and Charing Cross both ¾m, Waterloo 1m. Underground: Westminster ¼m.*

Westminster Abbey Chapter House

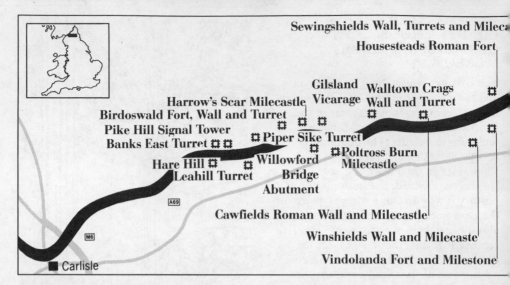

Sewingshields Wall, Turrets and Milec
Housesteads Roman Fort
Gilsland Walltown Crags
Vicarage Wall and Turret
Harrow's Scar Milecastle
Birdoswald Fort, Wall and Turret
Pike Hill Signal Tower
Banks East Turret
Piper Sike Turret
Poltross Burn
Milecastle
Hare Hill
Willowford
Leahill Turret Bridge
Abutment
Cawfields Roman Wall and Milecastle
Winshields Wall and Milecaste
Vindolanda Fort and Milestone
Carlisle

THE NORTHERN FRONTIER of Roman Britain stretched from the Solway Firth in the west to Wallsend in the east, until the building of the Antonine Wall. Between AD122 and 130 the Romans built 73 miles of forts, milecastles, turrets, signal towers and an immense wall. Once up to 20 feet high and nine feet wide, the wall was an outstanding piece of Roman military engineering.

Some 1,800 years later, much of Hadrian's Wall still exists and there is plenty to see along its whole length, which runs through some of England's most dramatic scenery.

Getting There by Bus or Train

West of Hexham the Wall roughly parallels the A69 Carlisle — Newcastle upon Tyne road, lying between 1 and 4 miles north of it, this road carrying an hourly bus service, Northumbria/CMS 685 Newcastle-Carlisle (Tel: 091-232 4211). The Newcastle-Carlisle railway line also has stations at Hexham, Haydon Bridge, Bardon Mill, Haltwhistle and Brampton. Closer access to the Wall is available on a special tourist bus from mid-July to early September linking Hexham and Haltwhistle stations and covering the section from Brunton Turret to Walltown Crags Turret on a hail-and-ride basis: Rochester & Marshall 890 (Tel: 0434 600263).

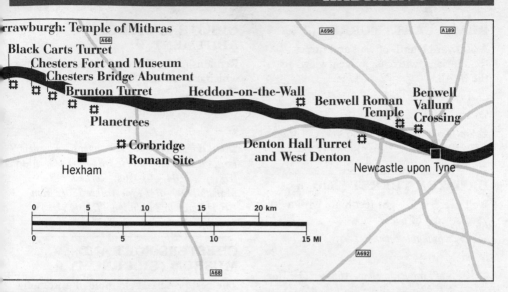

Brawburgh: Temple of Mithras
Black Carts Turret
Chesters Fort and Museum
Chesters Bridge Abutment
Brunton Turret
Heddon-on-the-Wall
Benwell Roman Temple
Benwell Vallum Crossing
Planetrees
Corbridge Roman Site
Denton Hall Turret and West Denton
Hexham
Newcastle upon Tyne

BANKS EAST TURRET (52a)

Well preserved with adjoining stretches of wall and fine views.

🕑 *Any reasonable time.*

🅿 ⊛

➡ *On minor road E of Banks village, 3½m NE of Brampton. (OS Map 86; ref NY 575647). Bus/Rail: See county introduction.*

BENWELL ROMAN TEMPLE

Remains of small temple, surrounded by modern housing.

🕑 *Any reasonable time.*

⊛

➡ *Immediately S off A69 at Benwell in Broomridge Ave. (OS Map 88; ref NZ 217646). Bus: Frequent from centre of Newcastle (Tel: 091-232 5325). Station: Newcastle 2m.*

BENWELL VALLUM CROSSING

An original causeway across the ditch giving access to a fort.

🕑 *Any reasonable time.*

⊛

➡ *Immediately S off A69 at Benwell in Denhill Park Ave. (OS Map 88; ref NZ 215646). Bus: Frequent from centre of Newcastle (Tel: 091-232 5325). Station: Newcastle 2m.*

BIRDOSWALD FORT, WALL AND TURRET

Important well-preserved fort on an escarpment with splendid views over the Irthing valley. Recent excavations of granaries and the west gate are exposed.

🕑 *Any reasonable time. (The site is in the care of Cumbria County Council who levy a charge for admission, reduced for EH members).*

⊛

✆ *(06977) 47602*

➡ *2¾m W of Greenhead, on minor road off B6318. (OS Map 86; ref NY 615663). Bus/ Rail: See county introduction.*

BLACK CARTS TURRET (29a)

A 500 yard length of wall and turret foundations, with magnificent views to the north.

Any reasonable time.

2m W of Chollerford on B6318. (OS Map 87; ref NY 884712). Bus/Rail: *See county introduction.*

BRUNTON TURRET (26b)

Well preserved, eight feet high, with a 70 yard stretch of wall.

Any reasonable time.

P

¼m S of Low Brunton on A6079. (OS Map 87; ref NY 922698). Bus: *Rochester & Marshall 890 (see above); also Tyne Valley 880/2 from BR Hexham (Tel: 0434 602217).* Station: *Hexham 4m.*

CARRAWBURGH: TEMPLE OF MITHRAS

Remains of a 3rd century temple and facsimiles of altars found during excavations. The originals are in the Museum of Antiquities, Newcastle.

Any reasonable time.

P

3¾m W of Chollerford on B6318. (OS Map 87; ref NY 869713). Bus/Rail: *See county introduction.*

CAWFIELDS ROMAN WALL AND MILECASTLE (42)

A dramatic section of wall with the land falling away in sheer crags to the north. The milecastle hangs on the edge.

Any reasonable time.

P

1¼m N of Haltwhistle off B6318 (OS Map 87; ref NY 716667). Bus/Rail: *See county introduction.*

CHESTERS BRIDGE ABUTMENT

Remains of the Roman bridge abutment which carried the Wall across the North Tyne river.

Any reasonable time.

On E bank of North Tyne opposite Chesters Fort, on footpath from B6318 (½m). (OS Map 87; ref NY 914700). Bus: *Rochester & Marshall 890, also Tyne Valley 880/2 from BR Hexham to within ½m (Tel: 0434 602217).* Station: *Hexham 4½m.*

CHESTERS FORT AND MUSEUM (CILURNUM)

The best preserved example of a Roman cavalry fort in Britain, including remains of the bath house on the banks of the River North Tyne. The museum houses a fascinating collection of Roman sculpture and inscriptions.

All year, plus Mondays in Winter. £1.80/£1.40/90p.

P

(0434) 681379

½m W of Chollerford on B6318. (OS Map 87; ref NY 913701). Bus: *Rochester & Marshall 890 (see above): also Tyne Valley 880/2 from BR Hexham to within ½m (Tel: 0434 602217).* Station: *Hexham 5½m.*

Chesters Fort

CORBRIDGE ROMAN SITE (CORSTOPITUM) ⚔

A fascinating series of excavated remains, including foundations of granaries with a grain ventilation system. From artefacts found, which can be seen in the site museum, we know a large settlement developed around this supply depot.

⏲ *All year. £1.80/£1.40/90p.*

⎁ ⫩ ⓟ ♿ ☻ ⑦ ⒢

☎ *(0434) 632349*

➠ *½m NW of Corbridge on minor road. (OS Map 87; ref NY 983649). Bus: Northumbria 602, 685 Newcastle-upon-Tyne — Hexham to within ½m (Tel: 091-232 4211). Station: Corbridge 1¼m.*

Lion and Stag Monument, Corbridge

DENTON HALL TURRET (7b) AND WEST DENTON ⚔

Foundations and 70 yard section of wall. The turret retains the base of the platform on which rested the ladder to the upper floor.

⏲ *Any reasonable time.*

☻

➠ *4m W of Newcastle city centre on A69. (OS Map 88; ref NZ 195656). Bus: Frequent from centre of Newcastle (Tel: 091-232 5325). Station: Blaydon 2m.*

GILSLAND VICARAGE ROMAN WALL ⚔

Two hundred and twenty yards of wall in the garden of a private house.

⏲ *Any reasonable time.*

☻

➠ *In former vicarage garden, Gilsland village. (OS Map 86; ref NY 632662). Bus/Rail: See county introduction.*

HARE HILL ⚔

A short length of wall standing nine feet high.

⏲ *Any reasonable time.*

☻

➠ *¾m NE of Lanercost, off minor road. (OS Map 86; ref NY 562646). Bus/Rail: See county introduction.*

HARROW'S SCAR MILECASTLE (49) ⚔

Remains linked to Birdoswald Fort by an impressive length of wall.

⏲ *Any reasonable time.*

☻

➠ *¼m E of Birdoswald Fort, 2¾m W of Greenhead, on minor road off B6318. (OS Map 86; ref NY 621664). Bus/Rail: See county introduction.*

HEDDON-ON-THE-WALL ⚔

A fine 280 yard stretch of wall, up to ten feet thick, with the remains of a medieval kiln near the west end.

⏲ *Any reasonable time.*

☻

➠ *Immediately E of Heddon village, S of A69. (OS Map 88; ref NZ 136669). Bus: Blue Bus 83E, OK 684, Northumbria 685 from Newcastle-upon-Tyne (Tel: 091-232 5325). Station: Wylam 3m.*

HOUSESTEADS ROMAN FORT (VERCOVICIUM)

Perched high on a ridge overlooking open moorland, this is the best-known part of the Wall. The fort covers five acres and the remains of many buildings, such as granaries, barrack blocks and gateways, can be seen. A museum displays altars, inscriptions and models.

⊙ *All year, plus Mondays in Winter. £1.80/ £1.40/90p.*

↟↟ P *(both on main road, ½m to S)* &. *(car park at site; enquire at NT/National Park information centre on main road)*

(*(0434) 344363*

➲ *2¼m NE of Bardon Mill on B6318. (OS Map 87; ref NY 790687). Bus/Rail: See county introduction.*

Housesteads Roman Fort

LEAHILL TURRET (51b)

Foundations of a turret originally constructed for the turf wall built before the stone wall.

⊙ *Any reasonable time.*

➲ *On minor road 2m W of Birdoswald Fort. (OS Map 86; ref NY 585653). Bus/Rail: See county introduction.*

PIKE HILL SIGNAL TOWER

The remains of a signal tower, 20 feet square, placed at an angle of 45 degrees to the Wall.

⊙ *Any reasonable time.*

P

➲ *On minor road E of Banks village. (OS Map 86; ref NY 597648). Bus/Rail: See county introduction.*

PIPER SIKE TURRET (51a)

A "Turf Wall" turret, built before the stone wall which abuts against the turret's east and west walls.

⊙ *Any reasonable time.*

➲ *On minor road 2m W of Birdoswald Fort. (OS Map 86; ref NY 588654). Bus/Rail: See county introduction.*

PLANETREES ROMAN WALL

A 50 feet length of narrow wall on broad foundations, showing extensive rebuilding in Roman times.

⊙ *Any reasonable time.*

➲ *1m SE of Chollerford on B6318. (OS Map 87; ref NY 928696). Bus: Rochester & Marshall 890, also Tyne Valley 880/2 from BR Hexham to within ¾m (Tel: 0434 602217). Station: Hexham 5½m.*

POLTROSS BURN MILECASTLE (48)

One of the best preserved milecastles, with part of a flight of steps to the top of the wall and the remains of gates, enclosing walls and barrack blocks.

⊙ *Any reasonable time.*

P *(near Station Hotel)*

➲ *Immediately SW of Gilsland village by old railway station. (OS Map 86; ref NY 634662). Bus/Rail: See county introduction.*

SEWINGSHIELDS WALL, TURRETS AND MILECASTLE (35) 🚶

A two mile section of wall, largely unexcavated, but preserving traces of a milecastle and turrets.

🕐 *Any reasonable time.*

♿

➡ *N of minor road, 1½m E of Housesteads Fort. (OS Map 87; ref NY 813702). Bus/Rail: See county introduction.*

VINDOLANDA FORT AND ROMAN MILESTONE 🚶

A fort and extensively excavated civil settlement covering 3½ acres. There is a museum which contains unusual artefacts of everyday Roman life.

🕐 *All year. (Access controlled by the Vindolanda Trust; EH members are admitted to site at half-price. Full price is payable if members visit the museum.)* £2.60/£1.80/£1.30.

🅿 ⛽ 👫 🅿 ♿

📞 *(0434) 344277*

➡ *1¼m SE of Twice Brewed, on minor road off B6318. (OS Map 87; ref NY 771664). Bus/Rail: See county introduction.*

Vindolanda Fort

WALLTOWN CRAGS WALL AND TURRET (45a) 🚶

A most impressive and well-preserved stretch of wall, 400 yards long, snaking over the Crags. The turret predates the wall and possibly formed part of a long-distance signalling system.

🕐 *Any reasonable time.*

🅿 *(nearby)* ♿

➡ *1m NE of Greenhead off B6318. (OS Map 87; ref NY 674664). Bus/Rail: See county introduction.*

WILLOWFORD BRIDGE ABUTMENT 🚶

One thousand yards of wall, including two turrets, leading to bridge abutment remains. This was much altered in Roman times owing to changes in the course of the river and consequent rebuilding of the bridge.

🕐 *Any reasonable time. (Access controlled by Willowford Farm; small charge levied.)*

♿

➡ *W of minor road ¾m W of Gilsland. (OS Map 86; ref NY 629664). Bus/Rail: See county introduction.*

WINSHIELDS WALL AND MILECASTLE (40) 🚶

One of the most rugged sections of the wall, about 350 yards long, including the highest point at Winshields Crag.

🕐 *Any reasonable time.*

♿

➡ *W of Steel Rigg car park, on minor road off B6318. (OS Map 87; ref NY 745676). Bus/Rail: See county introduction.*

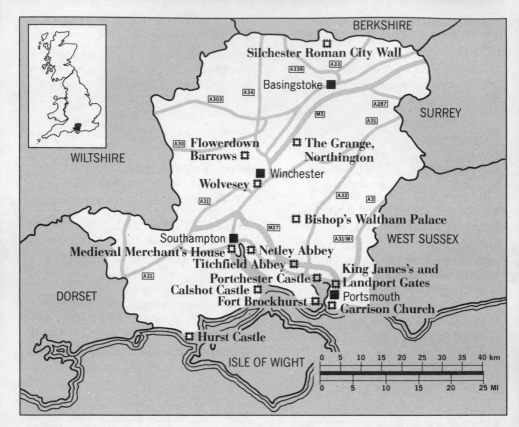

T HE COASTLINE OF HAMPSHIRE is dominated by the ports of Southampton and Portsmouth. Modern and thriving, they have been homes to both the Merchant and Royal Navies for many centuries. At the head of Portsmouth harbour lies Portchester Castle, with an almost perfect Norman keep and extensive Roman walls.

More recent are Hurst and Calshot Castles, built by Henry VIII as part of his coastal defences. Later still is Fort Brockhurst, one of a series built in the mid 19th century by Lord Palmerston to protect against invasion by the French.

To the east of Portsmouth, and running into Sussex are the South Downs. Noteworthy scenic points include Old Winchester Hill and Butser Hill. Nearby is Selbourne where the scenery has remained almost untouched since the time of Gilbert White. On the other side of the county lies the picturesque New Forest, famous for its ponies.

Further to the north lies Winchester, the centre of the county, and capital of Saxon Wessex. Near to its cathedral is the Bishop's Palace. The old medieval palace lies adjacent, where extensive ruins can still be seen.

⚑ BISHOP'S WALTHAM PALACE ⌂

This medieval seat of the Bishops of Winchester once stood in an enormous park. There are still wooded grounds surrounding the mainly 12th and 14th century remains we can see today. They include the Great Hall and three-storey tower, as well as the moat which once surrounded the palace. The ground floor of the Dower House is furnished as a 19th century farmhouse, with an exhibition on the powerful Winchester Bishops on the first floor.

🕐 *All year. £1.50/£1.10/75p.*

🚻 *(opposite car park on other side of main road)* 🅿 & *(grounds only)* ♿

✆ *(0489) 892460*

➲ *In Bishop's Waltham (OS Map 185; ref SU 552173). Bus: Hampshire Bus 69 Winchester-Southsea, Solent Blue Line 48A/C from Eastleigh (Tel: 0703 226235). Station: Botley 3½m.*

Bishop's Waltham Palace

⚑ CALSHOT CASTLE ⌂

Henry VIII built this coastal fort in an excellent position, commanding the sea passage to Southampton. The fort houses an exhibition and recreated pre-World War I barrack room.

🕐 *Summer season. £1.10/85p/55p.*

🅿 🚻 ♿

✆ *(0703) 892023*

➲ *On spit 2m SE of Fawley off B3053 (OS Map 196; ref SU 488025). Bus: Solent Blue Line X9, 39 Southampton-Calshot (passes BR Southampton) to within 1m (Tel: 0703 226235).*

Calshot Castle

FLOWERDOWN BARROWS ⌂

Round barrows of a Bronze Age burial site which were once part of a larger group.

🕐 *Any reasonable time.*

♿

➲ *In Littleton, 2½m NW of Winchester off A272 (OS Map 185; ref SU 459320). Bus: Hampshire Bus 31/2/4 from Winchester (pass BR Winchester) (Tel: 0962 852352). Station: Winchester 2m.*

FORT BROCKHURST ⚏

This was a new type of fort, built in the 19th century to protect Portsmouth with formidable fire-power. Largely unaltered, the parade ground, gun ramps and moated keep can all be viewed. An exhibition illustrates the history of Portsmouth's defences.

🕐 *All year. £1.50/£1.10/75p.*

📖 ♦♦ 🅿 ✪ ♿ *(grounds & ground floor only; ♦♦ for ♿)*

☎ *(0705) 581059*

➲ *Off A32, in Gunner's Way, Elson, on N side of Gosport (OS Map 196; ref SU 596020). Bus: Provincial 1-7, 37 Fareham-Gosport Ferry (pass BR Fareham, also Gosport Ferry links with BR Portsmouth & Southsea) (Tel: 0705 586921). Station: Fareham 3m.*

Fort Brockhurst

THE GRANGE, NORTHINGTON ⚏

This magnificent neoclassical country house, built at the beginning of the 18th century, could easily be mistaken for a Greek temple, with its vast portico front and grand steps.

🕐 *Any reasonable time (exterior viewing only).*

🅿 ♿ *(with assistance)* ✪

➲ *4m N of New Alresford off B3046 (OS Map 185; ref SU 562362). Station: Winchester 8m.*

⚑ HURST CASTLE ⚏

This was one of the most sophisticated fortresses built by Henry VIII, and later strengthened in the 19th and 20th centuries, to command the narrow entrance to the Solent. There is a castle exhibition and, outside, two huge 38 ton guns from the fort's armaments.

🕐 *Summer season, daily; Winter, weekends only, 10am-4pm. £1.50/£1.10/75p.*

♦♦ 🍴 ✪

☎ *(0590) 642344*

➲ *On Pebble Spit S of Keyhaven. Best approached by ferry from Keyhaven (OS Map 196; ref SZ 319898). Bus: Wilts & Dorset 123/4 Bournemouth-Lymington (passes BR New Milton) to within 2½m (Tel: 0202 673555). Station: Lymington Town 4½m to Keyhaven, 6½m to Fort.*

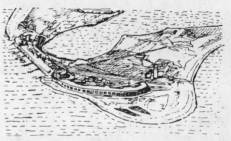

Hurst Castle

MEDIEVAL MERCHANT'S HOUSE, SOUTHAMPTON 🏛

The life of a prosperous merchant in the Middle Ages is vividly evoked by the brightly painted cabinets and chests, and colourful wall hangings authentically recreated for this faithfully restored 13th century town house, originally built as a shop and home for wine merchant John Fortin.

🕐 *All year. £1.80/£1.40/90p.*

⛹ 🎧 ♿ *(one step)* 🗎 ⊗

✆ *(0703) 221503*

➲ *58 French Street, ¼m S of city centre just off Castle Way (between High St and Bugle St) (OS Map 196; ref SU 419112). Bus: Southampton Citybus 17A/B, 27 from BR Southampton (Tel: 0703 553011). Station: Southampton ¾m.*

Medieval Merchant's House

NETLEY ABBEY 🏚

There is a peaceful and beautiful setting for the extensive ruins of this 13th century Cistercian abbey converted in Tudor times for use as a house.

⊕ Summer season, daily; Winter, weekends only, 10am-4pm. £1.10/85p/55p.

P &. ⊛

✆ (0703) 453076

➲ In Netley, 4m SE of Southampton, facing Southampton Water (OS Map 196; ref SU 453089). Bus: Southampton Citybus 16A/B, 17A/B. BR Southampton-Hamble (Tel: 0703 553011). Station: Netley 1m.

Netley Abbey

⚔ PORTCHESTER CASTLE 🏰

A residence for kings and a rallying point for troops, the history of this grand castle stretches back for 2,000 years. There are Roman walls, the most complete in Europe, substantial remains of the royal castle and an exhibition which tells the story of Portchester.

⊕ All year. £1.50/£1.10/75p.

P &. *(grounds & lower levels only)*
🚻 *in car park* ⊛ 🗋

✆ (0705) 378291

➲ On S side of Portchester off A27 (OS Map 196; ref SU 625046). Bus: Red Admiral 65/ A, 67 Fareham-Southsea to within ¼m (Tel: 0705 650967). Station: Portchester 1m.

Portchester Castle

PORTSMOUTH: ROYAL GARRISON CHURCH 🏚

Originally a hospice for pilgrims, this 16th century chapel became the Garrison Church after the Dissolution. Expertly restored in the 1860's but fire-bombed in 1941, the chancel survived and there is still plenty to see.

⊕ Keykeeper. Tel. (0705) 527667 for details.

P &. ⊗

➲ On Grand Parade S of Portsmouth High St (OS Map 196; ref SU 633992). Bus: From surrounding areas (Tel: 0705 650967). Station: Portsmouth Harbour ¾m.

English ⌗ Heritage

New exhibition at Portchester Castle

The 1,700 year history of Portchester Castle is unravelled at a major new exhibition — you can revolve a model of the Roman fort, open the coffin covers of three Saxon dead, look for a recipe in a medieval cook book, and even hear a French prisoner-of-war snoring in a hammock overhead! There are displays of jewellery, cooking pots and other objects found during archaeological digs, and a special tableau for children, with life-size figures telling lively stories from the medieval history of the castle.

Garrison Church

PORTSMOUTH: KING JAMES'S AND LANDPORT GATES ⌂

Now forming the entrances to the services' playing fields, for officers and other ranks respectively, these gates were once part of the 17th century defences of Portsmouth.

⊕ *Any reasonable time (exteriors only).*

⊛

➤ *King James's Gate: forms entrance to United Services Recreation Ground (officers) on Park Rd; Landport Gate: as above, men's entrance on St George's Rd (OS Map 196; King James's Gate ref SU 638000, Landport Gate ref SU 634998). Bus: From surrounding areas (Tel: 0705 650967). Station: Portsmouth Harbour ¼m.*

SILCHESTER ROMAN CITY WALLS AND AMPHITHEATRE ⚔

The tribal capital of Calleva Atrebatum, now possessing the most fully excavated and best preserved Roman town walls in Britain, almost 1½ miles around, and an impressive amphitheatre just outside the walls.

⊕ *Any reasonable time.*

⊛

➤ *1m E of Silchester (OS Map 175; ref SU 643624). Bus: Hampshire Bus 44 from Basingstoke (passes BR Bramley) to within 1m (Tel: 0256 464501). Station: Bramley or Mortimer, both 2¾m.*

TITCHFIELD ABBEY

Remains of a 13th century abbey overshadowed by the grand Tudor gatehouse built when the abbey was converted into a mansion for the Earl of Southampton after the Dissolution. Reputedly some of Shakespeare's plays were performed here for the first time.

⏱ *Any reasonable time.*

🅿 ⛐ ⚲

➡ *½m N of Titchfield off A27 (OS Map 196; ref SU 541067). Bus: Provincial 78A/B Fareham-Southampton, 79 Fareham-Hamble (Tel: 0705 586921). Station: Fareham 2m.*

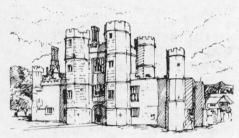

Titchfield Abbey

WOLVESEY: OLD BISHOP'S PALACE

The fortified palace of Wolvesey was the chief residence of the Bishops of Winchester and one of the greatest of all medieval ecclesiastical buildings. Its ruins still reflect the importance and immense wealth of the Bishops of Winchester, occupants of the richest see in medieval England.

⏱ *Summer season. £1.10/85p/55p.*

⛐ ⚲

📞 *(0962) 854766*

➡ *¼m SE of Winchester Cathedral, next to the Bishop's Palace; access from College St (OS Map 185; ref SU 484291). Bus: From surrounding areas (Tel: 0962 852352). Station: Winchester ¼m.*

Wolvesey: Old Bishop's Palace

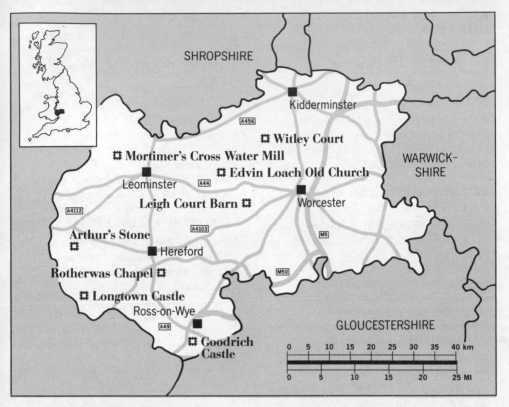

SHROPSHIRE

Kidderminster

A456

⌗ **Witley Court**

⌗ **Mortimer's Cross Water Mill**

⌗ **Edvin Loach Old Church**

Leominster   A44

WARWICK-
SHIRE

Leigh Court Barn ⌗

Worcester

A4112

Arthur's Stone
⌗

A4103

M5

■ Hereford

Rotherwas Chapel ⌗

M50

⌗ **Longtown Castle**

Ross-on-Wye

GLOUCESTERSHIRE

A49

⌗ **Goodrich
Castle**

0   5   10   15   20   25   30   35   40 km

0   5   10   15   20   25 MI

NOW ONE COUNTY, the identities of the two counties from which Hereford and Worcester is formed can still be clearly felt. It is bounded by Wales to its west and the Cotswolds to its east. With the River Wye in the south, running through Hereford and Ross-on-Wye, and the Wyre Forest near Kidderminster in the north, the county has retained a pleasant, tranquil atmosphere.

This is not reflected in the history of the county. Once part of the Kingdom of Mercia, the land was fought over for centuries. Along the county's Welsh border are two 12th century castles, Goodrich and Longtown, built as defensive positions from the Marcher Lords.

Near Leominster in the north lies Mortimer's Cross where a Water Mill now stands on the site of a decisive battle in the Wars of the Roses, which resulted in the defeat of the Lancastrians and the enthronement of Edward IV.

Built in the 18th century, the Mill was in use until the 1940's, and is still in working order. Near Worcester lies Leigh Court Barn, a magnificent 14th century timber-framed barn. More recent is Witley Court, a huge country house built in the Victorian Italianate style but now in ruins.

ARTHUR'S STONE, DORSTONE

Impressive prehistoric burial chamber formed of large blocks of stone.

⏲ *Any reasonable time.*

🚫

➡ *7m E of Hay-on-Wye off B4348 near Dorstone (OS Map 148; ref SO 319431).* Bus: *Red & White 39 Hereford-Brecon to within ¾m (Tel: 0633 265100).*

EDVIN LOACH OLD CHURCH

Peaceful and isolated 11th century church remains.

⏲ *Any reasonable time.*

🅿 🚫

➡ *4m N of Bromyard on unclassified road off B4203 (OS Map 149; ref SO 663585).*

GOODRICH CASTLE

This magnificent red sandstone castle is remarkably complete, with a 12th century keep and extensive remains from the 13th and 14th centuries. From the battlements there are fine views of the Wye Valley.

⏲ *All year. £1.50/£1.10/75p.*

🚻 🅿 🚫 🅰

✆ *(0600) 890538*

➡ *5m S of Ross-on-Wye off A40 (OS Map 162; ref SO 579199).* Bus: *Red & White/ Martin's 61 Monmouth — Ross-on-Wye to within ½m (Ross-on-Wye is linked with Hereford and Gloucester) (Tel: 0873 821241 and 0633 265100).*

LEIGH COURT BARN

Magnificent 14th century timber-framed barn, built for the monks of Pershore Abbey. It is the largest of its kind in Britain.

⏲ *Summer season: Thur-Sun 10am-6pm.*

🚫

➡ *5m W of Worcester on unclassified road off A4103 (OS Map 150; ref 784534).* Bus: *Midland Red West 417, 421, 422/3/5 from Worcester to within 1m (Tel: 0345 212 555).* Station: *Worcester Foregate Street 5m.*

LONGTOWN CASTLE

An unusual cylindrical keep built c.1200, with walls 15 feet thick. There are excellent views of the nearby Black Mountains.

⏲ *Any reasonable time.*

🚫

➡ *4m WSW of Abbey Dore (OS Map 161; ref SO 321291).*

Goodrich Castle

MORTIMER'S CROSS WATER MILL 🏚

The whole process of corn milling can be understood within this intriguing 18th century mill, still in working order.

⏱ *1 Apr-30 Sept: Thur, Sun and Bank Holidays only 2-6pm. £1.00/70p/50p.*

♿ *(exterior & ground floor only)* ⊗

➡ *7m NW of Leominster on B4362 (OS Map 148; ref SO 426637). Station: Leominster 7½m.*

Mortimer's Cross Water Mill

ROTHERWAS CHAPEL 🏛

This chapel, dating from the 14th and 16th centuries, is testament to the past grandeur of the Bodenham family and features an interesting mid-Victorian side chapel.

⏱ *Any reasonable time.*

🅿 ♿ *(kissing gate)* ⊗

➡ *1½m SE of Hereford on B4399 (OS Map 149; ref SO 537383). Bus: Hereford Hopper 110/1/8 from City Centre (Tel: 0345 212 555). Station: Hereford 3½m.*

WITLEY COURT 🏛

Spectacular ruins of a once great house. This vast mansion, in the Victorian Italian style, incorporates porticoes by John Nash and the nearby church, which has a remarkable 18th century baroque interior. The magnificent Poseidon fountain in the gardens will be operating on the first Sunday in the month from May to September.

⏱ *All year. £1.10/85p/55p.*

🅿 🚻 ⊗

☎ *(0299) 896636*

➡ *10m NW of Worcester on A443 (OS Map 150; ref 769649). Station: Droitwich Spa 8½m.*

Witley Court

Rotherwas Chapel

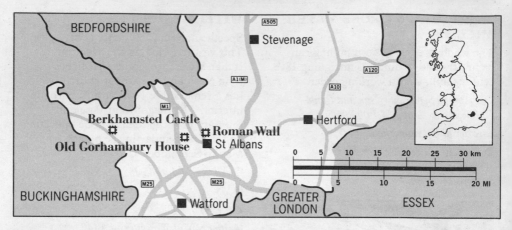

F OR CENTURIES, HERTFORDSHIRE has carried many of the main northern routes out of London. There is the prehistoric Icknield Way, as well as several Roman roads, including Akeman Street and Watling Street. St Albans, originally Roman and situated on Watling Street, still has parts of a Roman wall, mosaic tiled floors, an amphitheatre, and an abbey church.

BERKHAMSTED CASTLE

The extensive remains of a large 11th century motte and bailey castle which held a strategic position on the road to London.

◷ *Any reasonable time.*

✆ *(0442) 862411*

➲ *Adjacent to Berkhamsted station (OS Map 165; ref SP 996083). Bus: From surrounding areas (Tel: 0992 556765). Station: Berkhamsted.*

OLD GORHAMBURY HOUSE

Set in gently rolling farmland, the surviving remains of this Elizabethan mansion, particularly the porch of the Great Hall, illustrate the impact of the Renaissance on English architecture.

◷ *May-Sept, Thurs only 2-5pm, or at other times by appointment.*

✆ *(0727) 54051 (mornings only)*

➲ *¼m W of Gorhambury House & accessible only through private drive from A4147 at St Albans (2m) (OS Map 166; ref TL 110077). Bus: Hertsrider 300 St Albans-Hemel Hempstead to start of drive. (Tel: 0992 556765). Station: St Albans Abbey 3m, St Albans 3½m.*

ROMAN WALL, ST ALBANS

Several hundred yards of the wall, built c.AD200, which enclosed the Roman city of Verulamium, once the third largest town in Britain. The remains of towers and foundations of a gateway can still be seen.

◷ *Any reasonable time.*

➲ *On S side of St Albans, ½m from centre off A4147 (OS Map 166; ref TL 135067). Bus: From surrounding areas (Tel: 0992 556765). Station: St Albans Abbey ½m, St Albans 1¼m.*

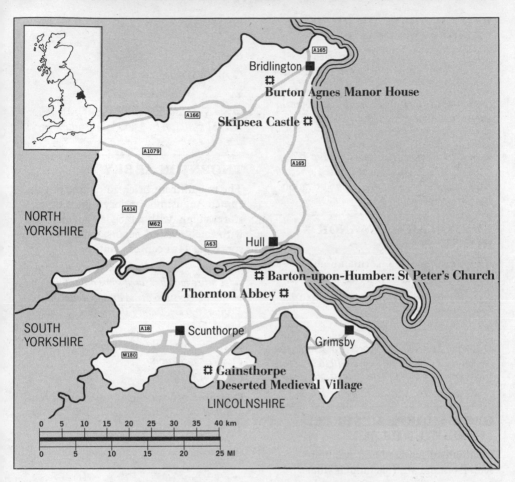

OR CENTURIES THE HUMBER has separated the East Riding of Yorkshire from Lincolnshire. Now it runs through the centre of the county of Humberside. But whatever the regional boundaries, the river has always been the area's life-blood.

The fishing port of Grimsby lies on the Humber's estuary; the rivers Trent, Aire, Don and Ouse all feed into it, and the once isolated town of Hull stands beside it, rejuvenated since the completion of the bridge.

Evidence of our forebears abounds. Place names map the successive invasions of the Romans, Saxons and Danes. Deserted medieval villages can be found — such as the one at Gainsthorpe. There is a considerable legacy of medieval building, including the rare Norman manor house at Burton Agnes. And a little south of Hull lie the 10th century churches of St Peter's, at Barton, and the magnificent 12th century abbey at Thornton.

BARTON-UPON-HUMBER: ST PETER'S CHURCH 🏛

A fine 15th century former parish church, with an Anglo-Saxon tower and baptistry.

⊙ *Mon-Fri 2-4pm. Weekends by appointment only — tel. Area Office: (0904) 658626.*

🌐

➲ *In Barton-upon-Humber. (OS Map 112; ref TA 034220). Bus: Road Car/E Yorks 350 Hull-Scunthorpe (Tel: 0482 27146). Station: Barton-upon-Humber ½m.*

BURTON AGNES MANOR HOUSE 🏠

A rare example of a Norman house, altered and encased in brick in the 17th and 18th centuries.

⊙ *All year.*

🌐

➲ *Burton Agnes village, 5m SW of Bridlington on A166. (OS Map 101; ref TA 103633). Bus: E Yorkshire 744 BR York-Bridlington (Tel: 0482 27146). Station: Nafferton 5m.*

GAINSTHORPE DESERTED MEDIEVAL VILLAGE

Originally discovered and still best seen from the air, this hidden village comprises earthworks of peasant houses, gardens and streets.

⊙ *Any reasonable time.*

🌐

➲ *On minor road W of A15 S of Hibaldstow 5m SW of Brigg (no directional signs). (OS Map 112; ref SK 955012). Station: Kirton Lindsey 3m.*

SKIPSEA CASTLE 🏰

The remaining earthworks of a Norman motte and bailey castle.

⊙ *Any reasonable time.*

🌐

➲ *8m S of Bridlington, W of Skipsea village. (OS Map 107; ref TA 163551). Bridlington 9m.*

THORNTON ABBEY 🏛

The magnificent brick gatehouse of this ruined Augustinian priory stands three storeys high, with a facade ornamented with finely-carved details, including some surviving 14th century statues.

⊙ *Summer season, daily, but gatehouse and sales office may be closed some days; telephone before your visit to avoid disappointment. Winter, weekends only 10am-4pm. £1.10/85p/ 55p.*

🅿 ♿ *(except interior of gatehouse and part of chapter house ruins)* 🎁 🌐

✆ *(0469) 40357*

➲ *10m NE of Scunthorpe on minor road N of A160. (OS Map 113; ref TA 115190). Station: Thornton Abbey ¼m.*

Thornton Abbey

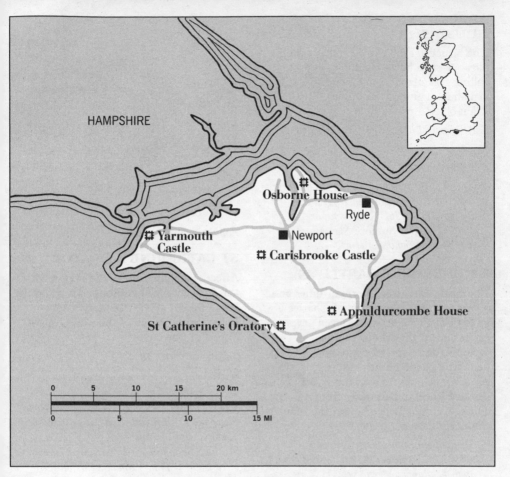

HAMPSHIRE

⌗ Osborne House

Ryde

⌗ Yarmouth Castle

■ Newport

⌗ Carisbrooke Castle

⌗ Appuldurcombe House

St Catherine's Oratory ⌗

```
0      5      10     15    20 km
0          5         10      15 MI
```

LOOK ACROSS POOLE BAY or the Solent towards the Isle of Wight from virtually anywhere between Swanage and Hurst Castle, and on a clear day you can see the brilliant white chalk headland of the Needles.

For centuries the Needles have been a beacon for sailors and yachtsmen, witnessing sad departures and triumphant returns. The Isle of Wight has many other headlands, making a picturesque coastline, bounding a remarkably varied island, which attracts thousands of people every year.

One of the island's highlights is Osborne House, built in the 1840's for Queen Victoria as a retreat from state ceremonial and where her children could enjoy a quiet country life near the sea. Osborne now stands as an unrivalled example of the domestic interior of the age to which she gave her name. Inland, near Newport, stands Carisbrooke Castle. Dating from Norman times, the view from its keep makes it possible to see virtually the whole island.

APPULDURCOMBE HOUSE ⚏ ✳

The bleached shell of a fine 18th century baroque-style house standing amidst a rolling green landscape in its own ornamental grounds, landscaped by 'Capability' Brown.

🕐 *All year. £1.10/85p/55p.*

⚭ 🅿 ♿ *(¼m walk uphill from car park)* ◉

✆ *(0983) 852484*

➥ *½m W of Wroxall off B3327 (OS Map 196; ref SZ 543800). Bus: Southern Vectis 2A Newport-Ventnor, 16B Ryde-Ventnor (Tel: 0983 62264). Station: Shanklin 3½m. Ferry: Ryde (Wightlink) 11m.*

Appuldurcombe House

⊠ CARISBROOKE CASTLE ⚏

The castle dates from Norman times and is best known as the prison of Charles I in 1647-8. There are some seven acres of castle and earthworks to explore, including the impressive gatehouse, the delightful chapel and the keep, and you can also see donkeys working a 16th century wheel to pull water from a well. The Governor's Lodge houses the island's County Museum.

🕐 *All year, plus Mondays in Winter. £3/ £2.30/£1.50. Families £8.50 (admits 2 adults & up to 4 children under 16 years).*

⚭ 🅿 🍽 *(April-Sept)* 👓 ♿ *(grounds & lower levels only)* 🗐 🌐 🚻 🗏 🗋

✆ *(0983) 522107*

➥ *1¼m SW of Newport (OS Map 196; ref SZ 486877). Bus: Southern Vectis 1B/C, 5C from East Cowes & Newport, 7/A from Yarmouth (Tel: 0983 62264). Station: Ryde Esplanade 9m. Ferry: West Cowes (Red Funnel) 5½m; Ryde (Wightlink) 8m; Yarmouth (Wightlink) 9m.*

ST CATHERINE'S ORATORY ⚏

Affectionately known as the Pepperpot, this 14th century lighthouse stands on the highest point of the island, erected following the wreck of the wine ship 'St Marie' of Bayonne.

🕐 *Any reasonable time.*

🅿 ◉

➥ *¾m NW of Niton (OS Map 196; ref SZ 494773). Bus: Southern Vectis 16/A/B Ryde-Newport, 17 Yarmouth-Ryde, to within ½m or 1m depending on route (Tel: 0983 62264). Station: Shanklin 9m. Ferry: West Cowes (Red Funnel) 14m; Yarmouth (Wightlink) 15m.*

Carisbrooke Castle

OSBORNE HOUSE

Queen Victoria's seaside home was built at her own expense in 1845 and designed by Thomas Cubitt. Here, she and Prince Albert sought peace and solitude, away from the affairs of state. At the request of their son, King Edward VII, this wonderful monument to Victorian family life has been preserved almost unchanged. The house itself is an Italianate villa with two tall towers. The apartments and rooms contain mementoes of royal travels abroad, sometimes incorporated into the decor. You will see intricate Indian plaster decoration, furniture made from deer antlers and over 400 works of art, pictures and pieces of furniture. The Royal Nursery on the top floor of the house, the miniature fortress built by 10-year old Prince Arthur in the gardens of the Swiss Cottage, and the Cottage itself, with fully furnished rooms set out as they were in 1854, are charming reminders of the early years of the royal children.

Summer season, grounds 10am-6pm, house open 10am-5pm (last admissions 4pm). 1-31 Oct, house & grounds open daily 10am-5pm (last admissions 4pm). £5/£4/£3.

Victorian carriage rides between house & Swiss cottage area. (exterior & ground floor only: vehicles with disabled passengers may set them down at house entrance before returning to car park)

((0983) 200022

1m SE of East Cowes (OS Map 196; ref SZ 516948). Bus: Southern Vectis 4 Ryde — E Cowes, 5 Newport — E Cowes (Tel: 0983 523831). Station: Ryde Esplanade 7m. Ferry: East Cowes (Red Funnel) 1½m; Ryde (Wightlink) 7m.

Osborne House

YARMOUTH CASTLE

This last addition to Henry VIII's coastal defences was completed in 1547 and is, unusually for its kind, square with a fine example of an angle bastion. It was garrisoned well into the 19th century. It houses an exhibition of paintings.

Summer season. £1.50/£1.10/75p.

(ground floor only)

((0983) 760678

In Yarmouth adjacent to car ferry terminal (OS Map 196; ref SZ 354898). Ferry: Yarmouth (Wightlink) adjacent.

Yarmouth Castle

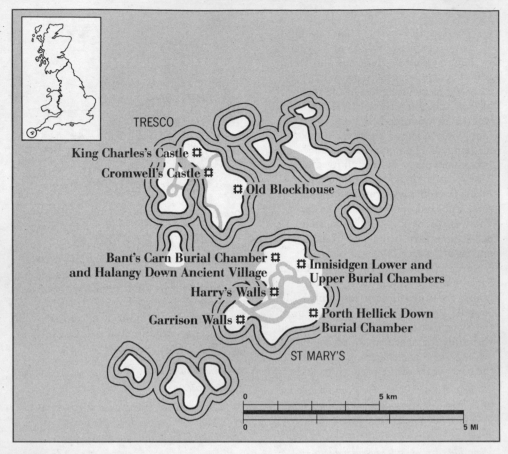

TRESCO

King Charles's Castle ⊞
Cromwell's Castle ⊞
⊞ Old Blockhouse

Bant's Carn Burial Chamber ⊞
and Halangy Down Ancient Village
⊞ Innisidgen Lower and
Upper Burial Chambers

Harry's Walls ⊞

Garrison Walls ⊞
⊞ Porth Hellick Down
Burial Chamber

ST MARY'S

0   5 km

0   5 MI

THE MOST WESTERLY inhabited outpost of the British Isles, facing the brunt of the Atlantic, the Scillies have played a surprisingly important role in English history.

In the Civil War the Scillies were one of the last Royalist strongholds. At the end of the 15th century, like so many strategic points along the south coast, the towns of St Mary's and Tresco were fortified with blockhouses and angled bastions. Later, in the 18th century, spectacular garrison walls were also added.

But the islands also have a much older history. Evidence survives of settlements by Neolithic, Bronze Age and Iron Age man: burial chambers, a mound and a village can all be visited.

But above all, the Scillies offer beautiful scenery: tiny harbours, isolated promontories, and gently undulating landscape. While the islands have a windy climate, they are never really cold, and are often a landfall for birds, some rare, blown far from other shores.

ST MARY'S: BANT'S CARN BURIAL CHAMBER AND HALANGY DOWN ANCIENT VILLAGE fi

In a wonderful scenic location, on a hillside above the site of the ancient Iron Age village, you will find this Bronze Age burial mound with entrance passage and chamber.

⏲ *Any reasonable time.*

☻

➡ *1m N of Hugh Town (OS Map 203; ref SV 911124).*

ST MARY'S: GARRISON WALLS ᛘ

You can take a pleasant walk along the ramparts of these well preserved walls and earthworks, built as part of the island's defences.

⏲ *Any reasonable time.*

☻

➡ *Around the headland W of Hugh Town (OS Map 203; ref SV 898104).*

ST MARY'S: HARRY'S WALLS ᛘ

An uncompleted 16th century fort intended to command the harbour of St Mary's Pool.

⏲ *Any reasonable time.*

☻

➡ *¼m NE of Hugh Town (OS Map 203; ref SV 910110).*

ST MARY'S: INNISIDGEN LOWER AND UPPER BURIAL CHAMBERS fi

Two Bronze Age cairns, about 100 feet apart, with stunning views over towards St Martins.

⏲ *Any reasonable time.*

☻

➡ *1¾m NE of Hugh Town (OS Map 203; ref SV 921127).*

ST MARY'S: PORTH HELLICK DOWN BURIAL CHAMBER fi

Probably the best preserved Bronze Age burial mound on the Islands, with an entrance passage and chamber.

⏲ *Any reasonable time.*

☻

➡ *1½m E of Hugh Town (OS Map 203; ref SV 929108).*

ᛘ TRESCO: CROMWELL'S CASTLE ᛘ

Standing on a promontory guarding the lovely anchorage between Bryher and Tresco, this 17th century round tower was built to command the haven of New Grimsby.

⏲ *Any reasonable time.*

☻

➡ *200yd W of King Charles's Castle, ¼m NW of New Grimsby (OS Map 203; ref SV 882159).*

ᛘ TRESCO: KING CHARLES'S CASTLE ᛘ

At the end of a bracing coastal walk to the northern end of Tresco you will find the remains of this castle built for coastal defence.

⏲ *Any reasonable time.*

☻

➡ *¼m NW of New Grimsby (OS Map 203; ref SV 882161).*

TRESCO: OLD BLOCKHOUSE ᛘ

The remains of a small 16th century gun tower overlooking the white sandy bay at Old Grimsby.

⏲ *Any reasonable time.*

☻

➡ *On Blockhouse Point, at S end of Old Grimsby harbour (OS Map 203; ref SV 898155).*

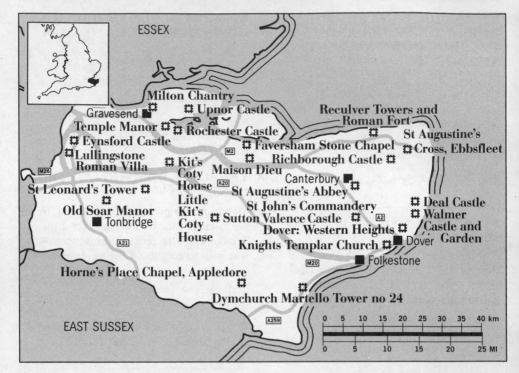

K ENT IS A PARADOX. The shortest route between England and the Continent, it has played host to invaders, travellers and visitors. Yet somehow the county remains extremely rural, with little villages and great tracts of countryside left largely untouched for centuries. The Weald and the North Downs contrast with the pretty grazing meadows of Romney, Hythe and the Isle of Sheppey.

But the story of the county is far from uneventful. Through war, invasion, conquest, woodland clearance and industrial development, a remarkable story book of Kent's chequered history survives.

The Romans built a villa at Lullingstone and there are some interesting remains of an amphitheatre at Richborough. You can see the foundations at Rochester Castle and a lighthouse in Dover which also both originate from Roman times.

From later periods there are also many religious sites, including St Augustine's Abbey, Faversham Stone Chapel and Horne's Place Chapel.

But most magnificent are Kent's castles: 11th century Rochester, Henry VIII's Deal and 16th century Upnor are just a few. At Dover, the castle includes Roman, Saxon, Norman and later additions — a reflection of the entire history of the county.

⟨X⟩ DEAL CASTLE ⊞

Crouching low and menacing, the huge, rounded bastions of this austere fort, built by Henry VIII, once carried 119 guns. It is a fascinating castle to explore, with long, dark passages, battlements, and a huge basement with an exhibition on England's coastal defences.

⊕ *All year. £1.80/£1.40/90p.*

⫟ ⌂ ⅋ *(courtyards & ground floor only)* ⊗

✆ *(0304) 372762*

➲ *SW of Deal town centre (OS Map 179; ref TR 378521). Bus: From surrounding areas (Tel: 0843 581333). Station: Deal ½m.*

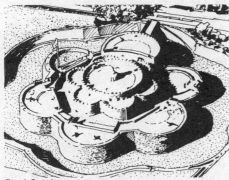

Deal Castle

⟨X⟩ DOVER CASTLE ⊞

Dramatically located on the white cliffs overlooking the English Channel, man and nature have combined to make this one of Western Europe's most impressive medieval fortresses. Its history is alive with reminders of a glorious past from the Iron Age to World War II. The great medieval keep towers to 95 feet and has walls up to 21 feet thick. There is also a rare Roman lighthouse, the remarkably restored Saxon church of St Mary of Castro, and ancient earthworks and tunnels, dating back to 1216. These are part of the defences, modernised through the centuries, of a castle which has played a key role in many historic events. Special attractions include Hellfire Corner (see page 86) and the "All the Queen's Men" Exhibition.

⊕ *All year, plus Mondays in Winter. £4.50/ £3.40/£2.30 (includes admission to Hellfire Corner).*

⌂ ⫟ ⓟ ⅋ *(for private functions tel. 0304 205830)* ⌕ *(underground works & keep)* ▤ ⅋ *(courtyard & grounds — some very steep slopes)* ⊗ ⌂

✆ *(0304) 201628*

➲ *On E side of Dover (OS Map 179; ref TR 326416). Bus: East Kent D77, 90/A from BR Dover Priory (Tel: 0843 581333). Station: Dover Priory 1½m.*

Dover Castle

DOVER CASTLE: HELLFIRE CORNER

It was from this amazing complex of tunnels and wartime operational rooms, concealed in the white cliffs beneath Dover Castle, that the evacuation in 1940 of troops from Dunkirk was masterminded. Originally excavated to house cannons to counter the threat of invasion by Napoleon and only recently removed from the top secret list, the tunnels are now open to the public for the first time.

Hellfire Corner is located within Dover Castle, for which opening hours and admission prices are listed on previous page. Admission to Hellfire Corner is by guided tour only, with last tours beginning at 5 pm in Summer and 3 pm in Winter.

☐ ¶ ♦♦ ⊗ &

Hellfire Corner

DOVER: KNIGHTS TEMPLAR CHURCH ⛪

Standing across the valley from Dover Castle are the foundations of a small circular 12th century church.

⊕ *Any reasonable time.*

⊛

➡ *On the Western Heights above Dover (OS Map 179; ref TR 313408). Station: Dover Priory ¾m.*

DOVER: WESTERN HEIGHTS ⛨

Parts of the moat of a 19th century fort built to fend off a French invasion and now incorporated into the White Cliffs Countryside Project.

⊕ *Any reasonable time.*

⊛ ℙ

➡ *Above Dover town on W side of Harbour. (OS Map 179; ref TR 312408). Station: Dover Priory ¾m.*

DYMCHURCH MARTELLO TOWER NO 24 ⛨

One of many artillery towers which formed part of a chain of strongholds intended to resist an invasion by Napoleon. It is fully restored, with an original 24-pounder gun on the roof.

⊕ *Keykeeper. Tel. (0424) 63792 for details.*

⊛

➡ *Access from High Street, not from seafront (OS Map 189; ref TR 102294). Bus: East Kent 11, 12 Folkestone-Hastings (pass close BR Folkestone Central) (Tel: 0843 581333). Station: Sandling 7m; Dymchurch (R H & D Rly), adjacent.*

Dymchurch Martello Tower No 24

EYNSFORD CASTLE

One of the first stone castles built by the Normans in the 11th century, the moat and remains of the curtain wall and hall can still be seen.

☉ *Any reasonable time.*

P & ⊛

➲ *In Eynsford off A225 (OS Map 177; ref TQ 542658). Bus: Kentish Bus 13 BR Eynsford-Dartford (Tel: 0474 321300). Station: Eynsford 1m.*

FAVERSHAM STONE CHAPEL

The remains of a small medieval church incorporating part of a 4th century Romano-British pagan mausoleum.

☉ *Any reasonable time.*

⊛

➲ *1¼m W of Faversham on A2 (OS Map 178; ref TQ 992614). Bus: Maidstone & District 333, 833 Maidstone-Faversham (pass BR Faversham) (Tel: 0634 832666). Station: Faversham 1½m.*

HELLFIRE CORNER
See Dover Castle.

HORNE'S PLACE CHAPEL, APPLEDORE

This 14th century domestic chapel was once attached to the manor house.

☉ *Wed only, 10am-5pm.*

P *(nearby)* ⊛

➲ *1½m N of Appledore (OS Map 189; ref TQ 957307). Station: Appledore 2½m.*

KIT'S COTY HOUSE AND LITTLE KIT'S COTY HOUSE

Ruins of two prehistoric burial chambers, taking their name from the Celtic phrase for 'tomb in the woods'.

☉ *Any reasonable time.*

⊛

➲ *W of A229 2m N of Maidstone (OS Map 188; ref TQ 745608 & 745604). Bus: Maidstone & District 101, 126 BR Maidstone East-Gillingham (Tel: 0634 832666). Station: Aylesford 2½m.*

LULLINGSTONE ROMAN VILLA

Some splendid mosaic tiled floors can be seen among the remains of this large country villa which has been extensively excavated in recent years. Four distinct periods of building have been identified as well as one of the earliest private Christian chapels.

☉ *All year. £1.50/£1.10/75p.*

⫩ P 🎧 ⊛

✆ *(0322) 863467*

➲ *½m SW of Eynsford off A225 (OS Map 177; ref TQ 529651). Station: Eynsford ¾m.*

Lullingstone Roman Villa

MILTON CHANTRY, GRAVESEND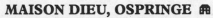

A small 14th century building which housed the chapel of the leper hospital and the chantry of the de Valence and Montechais families, and later became a tavern and in 1780 part of a fort.

🕐 *Keykeeper. Tel. (0634) 842852 for details.*

⊗

➡ *In New Tavern Fort Gardens E of central Gravesend off A226 (OS Map 177; ref TQ 652743).* Bus: *From surrounding areas (Tel: 0474 321300).* Station: *Gravesend ¾m.*

MAISON DIEU, OSPRINGE ⊞

This forerunner of today's hospitals remains largely as it was in the 16th century with exposed beams and an overhanging upper storey. It contains an exhibition about Ospringe in Roman times.

🕐 *Keykeeper. Tel. (0634) 842852 for details.*

🚻 ⊗

➡ *In Ospringe on A2 ½m W of Faversham (OS Map 178; ref TR 002608).* Bus: *Maidstone & District 333, 833 Maidstone-Faversham (pass BR Faversham) (Tel: 0634 832666).* Station: *Faversham ¾m.*

Milton Chantry

OLD SOAR MANOR, PLAXTOL ⊞

The remains of a late 13th century knight's manor house, comprising the two-storey solar (lord's private chamber) and chapel. There is an exhibition to visit.

🕐 *Summer season. (NT)*

⊗ 🅿 *(Limited)*

✆ *(0732) 810622*

➡ *1m E of Plaxtol (OS Map 188; ref TQ 619541).* Bus: *Maidstone & District 222 BR Borough Green-BR Tunbridge Wells, alight E end of Plaxtol, thence ¾m by footpath (Tel: 0634 832666).* Station: *Borough Green & Wrotham 2½m.*

Maison Dieu

Rochester Castle

RICHBOROUGH CASTLE ⚔

This fort and township date back to the Roman landing in AD43. The fortified walls and the massive foundations of a triumphal arch which stood 80 feet high still survive.

🕐 *All year. £1.40/£1/70p.*

🅿 ⚹ 🎧 ⊗ 🕊

☎ *(0304) 612013*

➡ *1½m N of Sandwich off A257 (OS Map 179; ref TR 324602). Station: Sandwich 2m. Riverbus (summer season only) from Highway Marine, Sandwich (Tel: 0304 613925).*

Richborough Castle

ROCHESTER CASTLE 🏰

Built in the 11th century to guard the point where the Roman road of Watling Street crossed the River Medway, the size and position of this grand Norman bishop's castle, founded on the Roman city wall, eventually made it an important royal stronghold for several hundred years. The keep is truly magnificent — over 100 feet high and with walls 12 feet thick. At the top you will be able to enjoy fine views over the river and surrounding city of Rochester.

🕐 *All year. £1.50/£1.10/75p.*

🚻 *(public, in castle grounds)* 🎧 ⊗ ⧆

☎ *(0634) 402276*

➡ *By Rochester Bridge (A2) (OS Map 178; ref TQ 742686). Bus: From surrounding areas (Tel: 0634 832666). Station: Rochester ½m.*

RECULVER TOWERS AND ROMAN FORT 🏰

This 12th century landmark of twin towers has guided sailors into the Thames estuary for seven centuries, but you can also see the walls of a Roman fort, which were erected nearly 2,000 years ago. It stands in a Country Park.

🕐 *Any reasonable time.*

🚻 🅿 ⚹ *(ground floor only — long slope up from car park)* ⊗

☎ *(02273) 66444*

➡ *At Reculver 3m E of Herne Bay (OS Map 179; ref TR 228694). Bus: East Kent/Regent 635, 645/6 from Herne Bay. (Tel: 0843 581333). Station: Herne Bay 4m.*

Reculver Towers

ST AUGUSTINE'S ABBEY, CANTERBURY 🏛

Founded in 598, this was one of the earliest monastic sites in southern England. Here you will find remarkable remains of the foundations of the original 6th century churches, the Norman church and medieval monastery.

🕓 *All year. £1.10/85p/55p.*

🚫 *(some steps)* 🔊 🅿 *(nearby)*

🕿 *(0227) 767345*

➡ *In Longport ¼m E of Cathedral Close (OS Map 179; ref TR 154578). Bus: From surrounding areas (Tel: 0843 581333). Station: Canterbury East & West, both ¾m.*

St Augustine's Abbey

ST AUGUSTINE'S CROSS, EBBSFLEET

A 19th century cross, in Celtic design, marking the traditional site of St Augustine's landing in 597.

🕓 *Any reasonable time.*

🚫 🔊

➡ *2m E of Minster off B2048 (OS Map 179; ref TR 340641). Bus: East Kent 611, 631 Ramsgate-Deal (Tel: 0843 581333). Station: Minster 2m.*

ST JOHN'S COMMANDERY, SWINGFIELD 🏛

A rare survival of a medieval chapel built by the Knights Hospitallers, ancestors of the St John Ambulance Brigade, which survived by being converted into a farmhouse in the 16th century. It has a fine moulded plaster ceiling and a remarkable timber roof.

🕓 *Contact Area Office on (0892) 548166 for details.*

🔊

➡ *2m NE of Densole off A260 (OS Map 179; ref TR 232440). Bus: East Kent 16 BR Folkestone Central-Canterbury to within 1m (Tel: 0843 581333). Station: Kearsney 4m.*

ST LEONARD'S TOWER, WEST MALLING 🏰

An early and fine example of a Norman tower keep, built c.1080 by Gundulf, Bishop of Rochester.

🕓 *Any reasonable time.*

🚫 *(grounds only)* 🔊

➡ *On unclassified road W of A228 (OS Map 188; ref TQ 675570). Bus: Maidstone & District 70 Maidstone-Borough Green (Tel: 0634 832666). Station: West Malling 1¼m.*

SUTTON VALENCE CASTLE 🏰

The ruins of a 12th century stone keep built to monitor the important medieval route across the Weald from Rye to Maidstone.

🕓 *Any reasonable time.*

🔊

➡ *5m SE of Maidstone in Sutton Valence village on A274 (OS Map 188; ref TR 815491). Bus: Maidstone & District 12, 812 Maidstone-Tenterden (pass BR Headcorn) (Tel: 0634 832666). Station: Headcorn 4m, Hollingbourne 5m.*

TEMPLE MANOR, ROCHESTER ⛪

The 13th century manor house of the Knights Templar which mainly provided accommodation for members of the order travelling between London and the Continent.

🕐 *Keykeeper. Tel. (0634) 842852 for details.*

🅿 ♿ *(grounds only)* ⊗

➡ *In Strood (Rochester) off A228 (OS Map 178; ref TQ 733686). Bus: From surrounding areas (Tel: 0634 832666). Station: Strood ¼m.*

Temple Manor

⚔ UPNOR CASTLE 🏰

This well preserved 16th century gun fort was built to protect Queen Elizabeth I's warships. However in 1667 it failed to prevent the Dutch navy which stormed up the Medway destroying half the English fleet.

🕐 *Summer season. £1.50/£1.10/75p.*

🚻 🅿 *(at a slight distance from castle — park before village)* ♿ *(grounds only)* ⊗

📞 *(0634) 718742*

➡ *At Upnor, on unclassified road off A228 (OS Map 178; ref TQ 758706). Bus: Maidstone & District 197 from BR Chatham. (Tel: 0634 832666). Station: Strood 2m.*

⚔ WALMER CASTLE AND GARDENS 🏰 ✱

This is one of the many forts built along the south coast by Henry VIII, and has since been transformed into an elegant stately home. As the residence of the Lords Warden of the Cinque Ports, Walmer was much used by the Duke of Wellington, and is still used today by HM the Queen Mother. Rooms used by Her Majesty including the dining room and drawing room, are open to visitors, as are those once used by Wellington, who died here. The delightful castle gardens should not be missed.

🕐 *All year, but closed Jan and Feb and when Lord Warden is in residence. £2.50/£1.90/ £1.30.*

🚻 🅿 🎧 ♿ *(courtyard & garden only)* ⊗ 📋

📞 *(0304) 364288*

➡ *On coast S of Walmer (OS Map 179; ref TR 378501). Bus: From surrounding areas (Tel: 0843 581333). Station: Walmer 1m.*

Walmer Castle

Upnor Castle

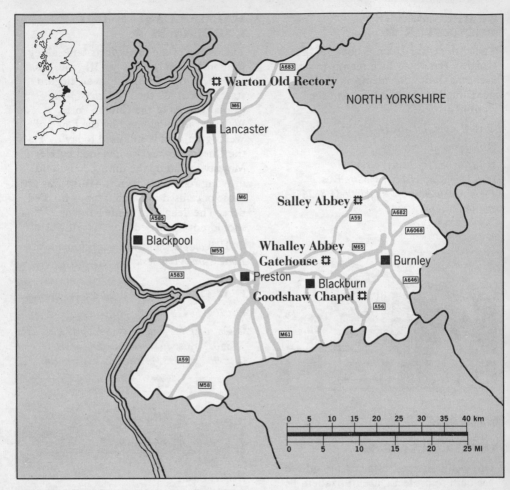

NORTH YORKSHIRE

Warton Old Rectory

Lancaster

Salley Abbey

Blackpool

Whalley Abbey
Gatehouse

Burnley

Preston

Blackburn

Goodshaw Chapel

0 5 10 15 20 25 30 35 40 km

0   5   10   15   20   25 MI

THIS IS A COUNTY which combines many aspects of English life, both past and present. It was at the vanguard of some of the earliest developments of the industrial revolution, including the creation of the cotton milling industry. The wealth it generated inspired and financed the confidence of the local Victorian architecture, and paid for local resort towns such as Blackpool.

Physically, the county is a contrast between its great milling towns and the wild open moorland of the Forest of Bowland, the Pennine frontier with West Yorkshire, and the expanse of Morecambe Bay, home to thousands of birds.

Earlier influences have also left their mark. The Cistercians founded important abbeys at Salley and Whalley, whose monks later played a leading role in the Pilgrimage of Grace, the great northern rebellion against the Dissolution in 1536.

GOODSHAW CHAPEL

A recently restored 18th century Baptist chapel with all its furnishings complete.

☉ *Keykeeper. Details at chapel or tel. Area Office: (0904) 658626.*

♿

➡ *2m N of Rawtenstall on minor road E of A682. (OS Map 103; ref SD 815263). Bus: Rossendale/Ribble 273 Burnley-Bolton; Ribble X43 Burnley-Manchester. All pass BR Burnley-Manchester Road. (Tel: 0772 263333). Station: Burnley-Manchester Road 4½m.*

SALLEY ABBEY

The remains of a Cistercian abbey founded in 1147.

☉ *All year.*

♿

➡ *At Sawley 3½m, N of Clitheroe off A59. (OS Map 103; ref SD 776464). Station: Clitheroe 4m.*

WARTON OLD RECTORY

A rare medieval stone house with remains of the hall, chambers and domestic offices.

☉ *All year.*

♿

➡ *At Warton, 1m N of Carnforth on minor road off A6. (OS Map 97; ref SD 499723). Bus: Ribble/Lancaster City 254/8 Lancaster-Warton (pass BR Carnforth) (Tel: 0772 263333). Station: Carnforth 1m.*

WHALLEY ABBEY GATEHOUSE

The outer gatehouse of the nearby Cistercian abbey. There was originally a chapel on the first floor, and side chambers flanking the gate passage.

☉ *Any reasonable time.*

♿

➡ *In Whalley, 6m NE of Blackburn on minor road off A59. (OS Map 103; ref SD 730360). Bus: Ribble 225 BR Blackburn-Clitheroe (Tel: 0772 263333). Station: Rishton 5½m.*

LEICESTERSHIRE

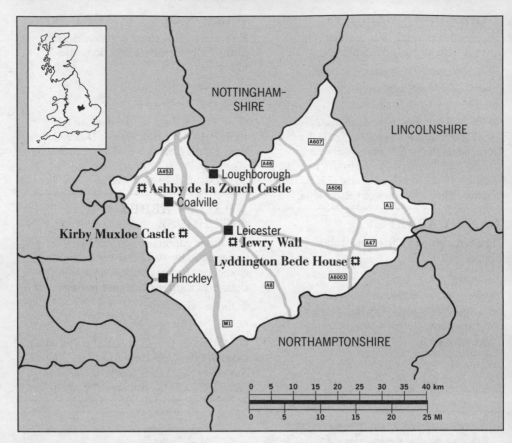

L EICESTERSHIRE IS A COUNTY of varied countryside. While much
of its earlier woodlands are now gone, small areas, such as Charnwood
Forest on its rocky upland, still survive. This contrasts with its soft,
undulating meadowlands, and wide views of the wolds, punctuated with widely
spaced villages.

Much of the form of the contemporary landscape has been moulded by the
needs of fox hunting, in which the county has a strong tradition. The wide
hedgerows and clumps of trees provide excellent cover.

At the centre of the county sits Leicester. Although a thriving modern city,
evidence of its Roman heritage still remains. The 30 feet high Jewry Wall is one of
the best in the country, originally designed to protect the original Roman city of
Ratae Coritanorum.

Near Leicester, at Kirby Muxloe and at Ashby de la Zouch, you can see the
remains of two castles, both built in the late 15th century by William, Lord
Hastings, Chamberlain to Edward IV.

94

ASHBY DE LA ZOUCH CASTLE ⛫

The impressive ruins of this late medieval castle are dominated by a magnificent tower, over 80 feet high, which was split in two during the Civil War, when the castle defended the Royalist cause.

⏱ *All year. £1.10/85p/55p.*

🅿 ♿ *(grounds only)* ⊛

✆ *(0530) 413343*

➲ *In Ashby de la Zouch, 12m S of Derby on A50 (OS Map 128; ref SK 363167). Bus: Stevensons 9, 27 Burton-on-Trent — Ashby de la Zouch: Midland Fox 118, 218 Leicester-Swadlincote (Tel: 0332 292200). Station: Burton-on-Trent 9m.*

Ashby de la Zouch Castle

KIRBY MUXLOE CASTLE ⛫

Picturesque, moated, brick-built castle begun in 1480 by William Lord Hastings. Potentially a residence of grandeur and considerable strength, it was left unfinished after Hastings was executed in 1483.

⏱ *All year. £1.10/85p/55p.*

🅿 ♿ ⊛

✆ *(0533) 386886*

➲ *4m W of Leicester off B5380 (OS Map 140; ref SK 524046). Bus: Midland Fox 63 from Leicester (Tel: 0533 511411): Leicester Citybus 152/3 from Leicester (Tel: 0533 514155). Station: Leicester 5m.*

LEICESTER: JEWRY WALL ⚓

One of the largest surviving lengths of Roman wall in the country. Over 30 feet high, it formed one side of the exercise hall of the civic baths.

⏱ *Any reasonable time.*

⊛

➲ *In St Nicholas St W of Church of St Nicholas (OS Map 140; ref SK 583044). Bus: From surrounding areas (Tel: 0533 514155 & 511411). Station: Leicester ¼m.*

LYDDINGTON BEDE HOUSE ⌂

Set among picturesque golden stone cottages, beside the handsome parish church of St Andrew, the Bede House was originally a medieval palace of the Bishops of Lincoln. It was later converted into an almshouse.

⏱ *Summer season. £1.10/85p/55p.*

⊛ ♿ *(ground-floor rooms only).*

✆ *(057282) 2438*

➲ *In Lyddington, 6m N of Corby, 1m E of A6003 (OS Map 141; ref SP 875970).*

Lyddington Bede House

Kirby Muxloe Castle

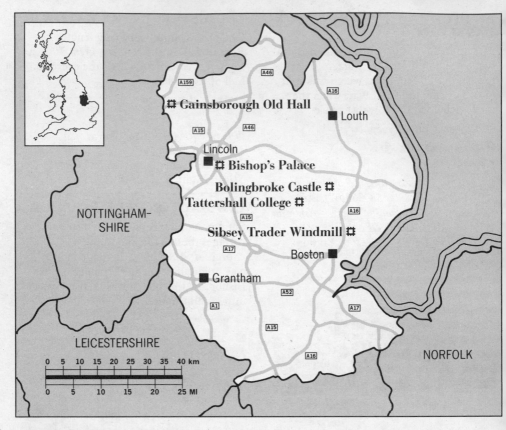

NOTTINGHAM-
SHIRE

⊞ Gainsborough Old Hall

■ Louth

Lincoln
■ **⊞ Bishop's Palace**

Bolingbroke Castle ⊞
Tattershall College ⊞

Sibsey Trader Windmill ⊞

Boston ■

■ Grantham

LEICESTERSHIRE

NORFOLK

| 0 | 5 | 10 | 15 | 20 | 25 | 30 | 35 | 40 km |

| 0 | 5 | 10 | 15 | 20 | 25 MI |

THE LOW-LYING PARTS of Lincolnshire, around the fens and dykes of the Wash are often referred to as 'Holland'. Consisting of silt and peat, they were mostly drained in the 17th century, which made them perfect for farming. Here, in the heart of the flatlands at Sibsey, you will find a 19th century windmill, its machinery still intact.

BISHOP'S PALACE, LINCOLN ⌂

In the shadow of Lincoln Cathedral are the remains of this medieval palace of the Bishops of Lincoln.

⏱ *Summer season. 75p/55p/40p.*

⊗ 🗎

✆ *(0522) 527468/532424*

➲ *S side of Lincoln Cathedral (OS Map 121; ref SK 981717).* Bus: *From surrounding areas (Tel: 0522 532424).* Station: *Lincoln 1m.*

Bishop's Palace

BOLINGBROKE CASTLE

Remains of a 13th century hexagonal castle, birthplace of Henry IV in 1367 and besieged by Parliamentary forces in 1643.

🕐 *Any reasonable time.*

🐕

➲ *In Old Bolingbroke, 16m N of Boston off A16 (OS Map 122; ref TF 349649). Station: Thorpe Culvert 10m.*

GAINSBOROUGH OLD HALL 🏛

A large medieval house with a magnificent Great Hall and suites of rooms. A collection of historic furniture and a re-created medieval kitchen are on display.

🕐 *1 April-31 October, Mon-Sat 10am-5pm, Sun 2-5.30pm. 1 Nov-31 March, Mon-Sat 10am-5pm. Closed Good Friday, 24-26 Dec, 1 Jan. £1.50/75p/75p (no reduction for students/unemployed).*

👬 🎧 ♿ *(most of ground floor)* ⊗ 🏛 ▯ ▯

☎ *(0427) 612669*

➲ *In Gainsborough, opposite the Library (OS Map 121; ref SK 815895). Bus: From surrounding areas (Tel: 0522 553135). Station: Gainsborough Central ½m, Gainsborough Lea Road 1m.*

Gainsborough Old Hall

SIBSEY TRADER WINDMILL 🌀

An impressive old mill built in 1877, with its machinery and six sails still intact. It can still be seen in action on occasions.

🕐 *Open on occasional Milling days (tel. 0246 823349 for details). 75p/55p/40p.*

👬 🅿 ♿ ⊗

➲ *½m W of village of Sibsey, off A16 5m N of Boston (OS Map 122; ref TF 345511). Station: Boston 5m.*

Sibsey Trader Windmill

TATTERSHALL COLLEGE 🏛

The remains of a grammar school for church choristers, built in the mid 15th century by Ralph, Lord Cromwell, the builder of nearby Tattershall Castle.

🕐 *Any reasonable time.*

⊗

➲ *In Tattershall (off Market Place) 14m NE of Sleaford on A153 (OS Map 122; ref TF 213577). Bus: Brylaine Boston-Woodhall Spa (passing close BR Boston) (Tel: 0205 364087). Station: Ruskington 10m.*

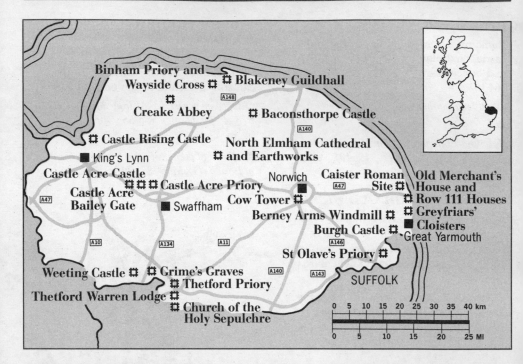

The map shows locations including: Binham Priory and Wayside Cross, Blakeney Guildhall, Creake Abbey, Baconsthorpe Castle, Castle Rising Castle, North Elmham Cathedral and Earthworks, King's Lynn, Castle Acre Castle, Castle Acre Priory, Norwich, Caister Roman Site, Old Merchant's House and Row 111 Houses, Castle Acre Bailey Gate, Cow Tower, Greyfriars' Cloisters Great Yarmouth, Swaffham, Berney Arms Windmill, Burgh Castle, St Olave's Priory, Weeting Castle, Grime's Graves, Thetford Priory, Thetford Warren Lodge, Church of the Holy Sepulchre, SUFFOLK. Roads labelled A148, A140, A47, A10, A134, A11, A146, A140, A143.

Scale: 0 5 10 15 20 25 30 35 40 km / 0 5 10 15 20 25 MI

MUCH OF NORFOLK, particularly around the Wash, lies just a few feet above sea level: the Fens in the west, marsh in the north, and the Broads and marshes in the east — noted for its abundance of birdlife. It's here that you will also find Berney Arms Windmill, one of the best and largest marsh mills in Norfolk.

By contrast, to the south in the heathland and forests of Breckland, there is an extensive group of Neolithic flint mines at Grime's Graves. The flint is now more visible as the building material used in much of the local housing.

In Roman times Norfolk was inhabited by the Iceni, and Roman remains can still be found at Caister, near Great Yarmouth. Great Yarmouth also has some fine 17th century houses and a 13th century Franciscan friary.

There are also several important castles near King's Lynn, including Castle Rising and Castle Acre — where there are also the remains of a 12th century Cluniac priory.

BACONSTHORPE CASTLE

The remains of the gatehouses of a large 15th century fortified manor house, partly surrounded by a lake.

⏲ *Any reasonable time.*

🅿 ♿

➜ *¾m N of village of Baconsthorpe off unclassified road 3m E of Holt (OS Map 133; ref TG 122382). Station: Sheringham 4½m.*

BERNEY ARMS WINDMILL 🌀

A wonderfully situated marsh mill, one of the best and largest remaining in Norfolk, with seven floors, making it a landmark for miles around. It was in use until 1951.

🕐 *Summer season. 75p/55p/40p.*

🚫

✆ *(0493) 700605*

➥ *3½m NE of Reedham on N bank of River Yare. Accessible by boat, by train to Berney Arms station (¼m walk) or by footpath from Halvergate (3½m) (OS Map 134; ref TG 465051). Station: Berney Arms ¼m.*

BINHAM PRIORY 🏚

Extensive remains of a Benedictine priory, of which the original nave of the church still continues in use as the parish church.

🕐 *Any reasonable time.*

🚫

➥ *¼m NW of village of Binham-on-Wells road off B1388 (OS Map 132; ref TF 982399).*

BINHAM WAYSIDE CROSS

Medieval cross marking the site of an annual fair held until the 1950's.

🕐 *Any reasonable time.*

🚫

➥ *On village green adjacent to Priory (OS Map 132; ref TF 982399).*

BLAKENEY GUILDHALL 🏛

The surviving basement, most likely used for storage, of a large 14th century building, probably a merchant's house.

🕐 *Any reasonable time.*

🚫

➥ *In Blakeney off A149 (OS Map 133; ref TG 030441). Station: Sheringham 9m.*

Berney Arms Windmill

BURGH CASTLE 🏛

Impressive walls, with projecting bastions, of a Roman fort built in the late 3rd century as one of a chain to defend the coast against Saxon raiders.

🕐 *Any reasonable time.*

🚫

➥ *At far W end of Breydon Water, on unclassified road 3m W of Great Yarmouth (OS Map 134; ref TG 475046). Bus: Eastern Counties 216/9 from Great Yarmouth (Tel: 0493 842341). Station: Great Yarmouth 5m.*

CAISTER ROMAN SITE 🏛

The remains of a Roman site, possibly a fort, revealed by excavation, including part of a defensive wall, a gateway and buildings along a main street.

🕐 *Any reasonable time.*

🚫

➥ *Near Caister-on-Sea, 3m N of Great Yarmouth (OS Map 134; ref TG 518125). Bus: Great Yarmouth Transport 8, 15-17 Eastern Counties 622/3/5/6, 701/5, 717/8 (Tel: 0603 613613). Station: Great Yarmouth 3m.*

CASTLE ACRE: BAILEY GATE 🏰

The north gateway to the medieval planned town of Acre with rounded flint towers.

🕐 *Any reasonable time.*

🌐

➡ *In Castle Acre, at E end of Stocks Green, 5m N of Swaffham (OS Map 132; ref TF 817152).*

CASTLE ACRE CASTLE 🏰

The remains of a Norman manor house, which became a castle, with earthworks, set on a hill by the side of the village.

🕐 *Any reasonable time.*

🌐

➡ *At E end of Castle Acre 5m N of Swaffham (OS Map 132; ref TF 819152).*

CASTLE ACRE PRIORY 🏛

The great west front of the 12th century church of this Cluniac priory still rises to its full height and is elaborately decorated. Other substantial remains include the splendid prior's lodgings and chapel, and the delightful walled herb garden should not be missed.

🕐 *All year. £1.80/£1.40/90p.*

🚻 🅿 🎧 ♿ *(ground floor & grounds only)* 🌐 📦

☎ *(0760) 755394*

➡ *¼m W of village of Castle Acre, 5m N of Swaffham (OS Map 132; ref TF 814148).*

CASTLE RISING CASTLE 🏰

A fine mid 12th century domestic keep, set in the centre of massive defensive earthworks. The keep walls stand to their original height and many of the fortifications are still intact.

🕐 *All year. £1.10/85p/55p.*

🗋 🚻 🅿 ♿ *(exterior only; 🚻 for ♿)* 🌐

☎ *(0553) 631330*

➡ *4m NE of King's Lynn off A149 (OS Map 132; ref TF 666246). Bus: Eastern Counties 410/1 King's Lynn-Hunstanton (Tel: 0553 772343). Station: King's Lynn 4½m.*

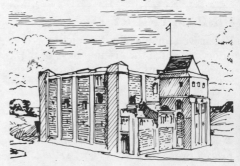

Castle Rising Castle

Castle Acre Priory

CREAKE ABBEY

The ruins of the church of an Augustinian abbey which suffered arson and plague before its eventual demise in the 16th century.

⊙ *Any reasonable time.*

⊛

➡ *1m N of North Creake off B1355 (OS Map 132; ref TF 856395).*

GREAT YARMOUTH: OLD MERCHANT'S HOUSE, ROW 111 HOUSES AND GREYFRIARS' CLOISTERS

Two 17th century Row Houses, a type of building unique to Great Yarmouth, containing original fixtures and displays of local architectural fittings salvaged from bombing in 1942-43. Nearby are the remains of a Franciscan friary, with a rare vaulted cloister, accidentally discovered during bomb damage repairs.

⊙ *Summer season. Entry by tour only. £1.10/ 85p/55p.*

⊛

☎ *(0493) 857900*

➡ *Great Yarmouth, on South Quay ½m inland from beach (OS Map 134; Houses ref TG 525072; Cloisters ref TG 525073). Bus: From surrounding areas (Tel: 0493 842341).* Station: *Great Yarmouth ½m.*

Old Merchant's House

GRIME'S GRAVES

These remarkable Neolithic flint mines, unique in England, comprise over 300 pits and shafts. The visitor can descend some 30 feet by ladder into one excavated shaft, and look along the radiating galleries from where the flint used to make axes and knives was extracted.

⊙ *All year. £1.10/85p/55p.*

🅿 ♿ *(exhibition area only; access track rough)* ⊛

☎ *(0842) 810656*

➡ *7m NW of Thetford off A134 (OS Map 144; ref TL 818898).* Station: *Brandon 3½m.*

Grime's Graves

NORTH ELMHAM CHAPEL

The remains of a Norman chapel converted into a fortified dwelling and enclosed by earthworks in the late 14th century by the notorious Bishop of Norwich, Hugh le Despencer.

⊙ *Any reasonable time.*

⊛

➡ *6m N of East Dereham on B1110 (OS Map 132; ref TF 988217).*

NORWICH: COW TOWER ⛫

A circular brick tower, which once formed part of the 14th century city defences, now standing alone in a delightful riverside setting.

⊙ *Any reasonable time.*

⊗

➜ *In Norwich, near cathedral (OS Map 134; ref TG 240091).* Bus: *From surrounding areas (Tel: 0603 761212).* Station: *Norwich ½m.*

ST OLAVE'S PRIORY ⛪

Remains of an Augustinian priory founded nearly 200 years after the death in 1030 of the patron saint of Norway after whom it was named. Several other churches in Norfolk are dedicated to King Olaf II of Norway who attempted to complete the conversion of his country to Christianity.

⊙ *Any reasonable time.*

⊛

➜ *5½m SW of Great Yarmouth on A143 (OS Map 134; ref TM 459996).* Station: *Haddiscoe 1¼m.*

THETFORD: CHURCH OF THE HOLY SEPULCHRE ⛪

The ruined nave of a priory church of the Canons of the Holy Sepulchre, named after the famous church in Jerusalem and the only surviving remains in England of a house of this order.

⊙ *Any reasonable time.*

⊛

➜ *On W side of Thetford off B1107 (OS Map 144; ref TL 865831).* Bus: *From surrounding areas (Tel: 0603 613613).* Station: *Thetford ¾m.*

THETFORD PRIORY ⛪

The 14th century gatehouse is the best preserved part of this Cluniac priory built in 1103. The extensive remains also include the complete plan of the cloisters.

⊙ *Any reasonable time.*

⊛

➜ *On W side of Thetford near station (OS Map 144; ref TL 865836).* Bus: *From surrounding areas (Tel: 0603 613613).* Station: *Thetford ¼m.*

THETFORD WARREN LODGE ⌂

The ruins of a small, two-storeyed medieval house, set in pleasant woods, which was probably the home of the priory's gamekeeper.

⊙ *Any reasonable time.*

⊛

➜ *2m W of Thetford off B1107 (OS Map 144; ref TL 839841).* Bus: *Eastern Counties 131/2 Bury St Edmunds-Brandon (pass close BR Thetford) (Tel: 0473 265676).* Station: *Thetford 2½m.*

WEETING CASTLE ⛫

The ruins of an early medieval manor house within a shallow rectangular moat.

⊙ *Any reasonable time.*

⊛

➜ *2m N of Brandon off B1106 (OS Map 144; ref TL 778891).* Station: *Brandon 1½m.*

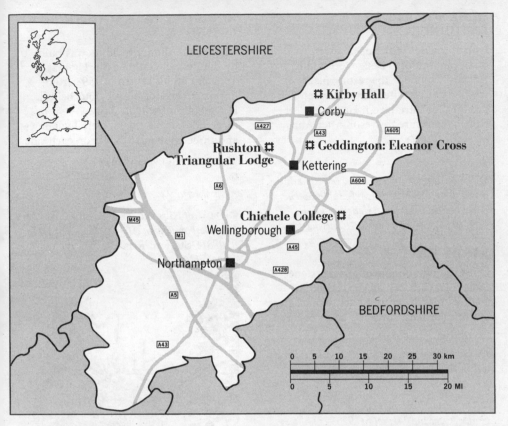

LEICESTERSHIRE

⌗ **Kirby Hall**
■ Corby

A427   A43   A605

⌗ **Geddington: Eleanor Cross**

Rushton ⌗
Triangular Lodge
■ Kettering

A6   A604

M45

Chichele College ⌗

M1   Wellingborough ■

A45

Northampton ■   A428

A5

BEDFORDSHIRE

A43

0	5	10	15	20	25	30 km
0	5		10		15	20 MI

A T ONE TIME, the ancient Rockingham Forest may have run right across Northamptonshire from Kettering in the south, north-eastwards towards Lincolnshire. It would probably have surrounded all the English Heritage properties, including the Elizabethan Kirby Hall and the mysterious triangular lodge at Rushton. Today, the county is largely given over to farming, with only a few parts of forest remaining.

From medieval times the leather industry has been important, as well as iron smelting. But without any natural coal, Northamptonshire escaped major industrialisation and still remains fundamentally a rural county.

CHICHELE COLLEGE

Parts of a quadrangle, incorporating a chapel, remain of this college for secular canons, founded by the Archbishop of Canterbury in 1422.

⏱ *Any reasonable time (exterior only).*

➲ *In Higham Ferrers, on A6 (OS Map 153; ref SP 960687).* Bus: *United Counties 46/A, X94 from Wellingborough (Tel: 0604 36681).* Station: *Wellingborough 5m.*

ELEANOR CROSS, GEDDINGTON

One of a series of famous crosses, of elegant sculpted design, erected by Edward I to mark the resting places of the body of his wife, Eleanor, when brought for burial from Harby in Nottinghamshire to Westminster Abbey.

Any reasonable time.

In Geddington, off A43 between Kettering and Corby (OS Map 141; ref SP 896830). Bus: *United Counties 8 Kettering-Corby. (Tel: 0604 36681).* Station: *Kettering 4m.*

KIRBY HALL

Outstanding example of a large, stone-built Elizabethan mansion, begun in 1570 with 17th century alterations. There are fine gardens, currently being restored.

All year. £1.10/85p/55p.

P *(grounds, gardens & ground floor only)*

(0536) 203230

On unclassified road off A43 4m NE of Corby (OS Map 141; ref SP 926927).

Kirby Hall

RUSHTON TRIANGULAR LODGE

This extraordinary building was built by the Roman Catholic Sir Thomas Tresham on his return in 1593 from imprisonment for his religious beliefs. It symbolises the Holy Trinity — it has three sides, three floors, trefoil windows and three triangular gables on each side.

Summer season. £1.10/85p/55p.

(0536) 710761

1m W of Rushton, on unclassified road 3m from Desborough on A6 (OS Map 141; ref SP 830831). Station: *Kettering 5m.*

Rushton Triangular Lodge

NORTHUMBERLAND

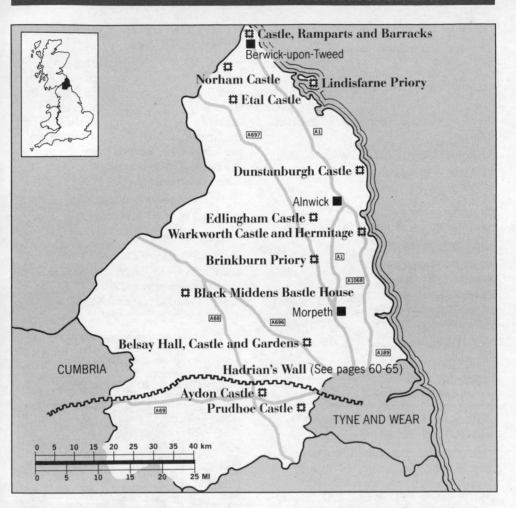

⚏ **Castle, Ramparts and Barracks**
■ Berwick-upon-Tweed
⚏ **Norham Castle**   ⚏ **Lindisfarne Priory**
⚏ **Etal Castle**

A697   A1

Dunstanburgh Castle ⚏
Alnwick ■
Edlingham Castle ⚏
Warkworth Castle and Hermitage ⚏
Brinkburn Priory ⚏   A1
A1068
⚏ **Black Middens Bastle House**
Morpeth ■
A68   A696
Belsay Hall, Castle and Gardens ⚏
A189
CUMBRIA   **Hadrian's Wall** (See pages 60-65)
⚏ **Aydon Castle**
Prudhoe Castle ⚏
A69   TYNE AND WEAR

0 5 10 15 20 25 30 35 40 km
0 5 10 15 20 25 MI

THE SHIFTING BORDER of Scotland has made Northumberland a disputed frontier for centuries. The Romans built Hadrian's Wall, and in the Middle Ages castles like Berwick and Norham were constructed to protect the border.

But as conflict gave way to stability and peace, the noble families built more elegant homes. These can best be seen at Warkworth and at Belsay, where the 13th century castle was replaced by a mansion in the 17th century, and once again in the early 19th century by an important neo-classical house.

At Lindisfarne there are the evocative ruins of the 11th century priory, still a destination of modern-day pilgrims. Lindisfarne also lies on one of the most beautiful stretches of Britain's coastline, rich in bird life, fishing villages and unspoilt beaches.

105

AYDON CASTLE ⌂

One of the finest fortified manor houses in England, dating from the late 13th century and situated in a position of great natural beauty. Its survival, remarkably intact, can be attributed to its conversion to a farmhouse in the 17th century.

⌚ *Summer season. £1.50/£1.10/75p.*

☐ ♦♦ 🅿 ♿ *(ground floor)* ▤ ⊗

☎ *(0434) 632450*

➡ *1m NE of Corbridge, on minor road off B6321 or A68. (OS Map 87; ref NZ 002663). Station: Corbridge 4m.*

Aydon Castle

BELSAY HALL, CASTLE AND GARDENS 🏠 ⌂ ✿

One of the most important neoclassical houses in Britain, completed in 1815, together with a well preserved 14th century castle and a ruined 17th century mansion. It has 30 acres of magnificent landscaped parkland and gardens, including the famous quarry gardens.

⌚ *All year. £2.10/£1.60/£1.10.*

☐ ♦♦ 🅿 ♿ *(grounds only; ♦♦ for ♿)* ☐ ▤ ⊗ ¶

☎ *(0661) 881636*

➡ *14m NW of Newcastle on A696. (OS Map 88; ref NZ 088785). Bus: National Express 370 Newcastle-Edinburgh to within 1m. (Tel: Any National Express agent). Station: Morpeth 10m.*

BERWICK-UPON-TWEED BARRACKS ⌂

Among the earliest purpose-built barracks, these have changed very little since 1717. They house an exhibition 'By Beat of Drum,' which recreates scenes such as a barrack room from the life of the British infantryman, the Museum of the Kings Own Scottish Borderers and the Borough Museum with fine art and other collections.

⌚ *All year. £1.80/£1.40/90p.*

♦♦ 🅿 ⊗ ⓜ ☐

☎ *(0289) 304493*

➡ *On the Parade, off Church St, Berwick town centre. (OS Map 75; ref NT 994535). Bus: From surrounding areas (Tel: 0289 307283 & 307461). Station: Berwick-upon-Tweed ¼m.*

Berwick Barracks

Belsay Hall

BERWICK-UPON-TWEED CASTLE ⚔

Largely destroyed when the railway station was built, there are still some remains of this 12th century castle, adjacent to the majestic Royal Border Bridge.

⏱ *Any reasonable time.*

🚻

➡ *Adjacent to Berwick railway station, W of town centre, accessible also from river bank. (OS Map 75; ref NT 994535). Bus: From surrounding areas (Tel: 0289 307283 & 307461). Station: Berwick-upon-Tweed, adjacent.*

BERWICK-UPON-TWEED RAMPARTS ⚔

A remarkably complete system of town fortifications, consisting of gateways, ramparts and projecting bastions, built in the late 16th century.

⏱ *Any reasonable time.*

♿ *(⚍ & 🅿 in town centre)* 🚻

➡ *Surrounding Berwick town centre on N bank of River Tweed. (OS Map 75; ref NT 994535). Bus: From surrounding areas (Tel: 0289 307283 & 307461). Station: Berwick-upon-Tweed ¼m.*

BLACK MIDDENS BASTLE HOUSE ⚔

A 16th century two-storey defended farmhouse, of a type peculiar to the Border regions, set in splendid walking country.

⏱ *Any reasonable time.*

🅿 🍴 🚻

➡ *200yds N of minor road 7m NW of Bellingham; access also along minor road from A68. (OS Map 80; ref NY 774900).*

BRINKBURN PRIORY ⛪

This late 12th century church is a fine example of early Gothic architecture, almost perfectly preserved, and is set in a lovely spot beside the River Coquet.

⏱ *Summer season. £1.10/85p/55p.*

🅿 🍴 *(short walk from 🅿)* 🚻

✆ *(0665) 570628*

➡ *4½m SE of Rothbury off B6334. (OS Map 81; ref NZ 116984). Bus: Northumbria 514/6 Morpeth-Rothbury to within ½m (Tel: 091-232 4211). Station: Acklington 10m.*

Brinkburn Priory

CHESTERS FORT AND MUSEUM 🍴

CORBRIDGE ROMAN SITE 🍴

See Hadrian's Wall section, pages 60-65.

DUNSTANBURGH CASTLE

An easy, but bracing, coastal walk leads to the eerie skeleton of this wonderful 14th century castle sited on a basalt crag, rearing up more than 100 feet from the waves crashing on the rocks below. The surviving ruins include the large gatehouse, which later became the keep, and curtain walls.

All year. £1.10/85p/55p. (NT)

(0665) 576231

8m NE of Alnwick, on footpaths from Craster or Embleton. (OS Map 75; ref NU 258220). Bus: *Northumbria 501 Alnwick — Berwick-upon-Tweed (passes close BR Berwick-upon-Tweed) with connections from Newcastle (passing Tyne & Wear Metro Haymarket), alight Craster, 1½m (Tel: 091-232 4211).* Station: *Chathill 7m, Alnmouth 8m.*

Dunstanburgh Castle

EDLINGHAM CASTLE

In a remote and picturesque valley, set beside a splendid railway viaduct, this complex ruin has defensive features spanning the 13th-15th centuries.

Any reasonable time.

At E end of Edlingham village, on minor road off B6341 6m SW of Alnwick. (OS Map 81; ref NU 115092). Station: *Alnmouth 9m.*

ETAL CASTLE

A compact 14th century border castle standing at the end of the village street, with a well preserved keep and gatehouse.

Any reasonable time.

(in village)

In Etal village, 10m SW of Berwick. (OS Map 75; ref NT 925394). Bus: *Taxibus 267 Berwick-upon-Tweed — Wooler (Tel: 0289 307588).* Station: *Berwick-upon-Tweed 10½m.*

HADRIAN'S WALL

See pages 60-65.

HOUSESTEADS ROMAN FORT

See Hadrian's Wall section, pages 60-65.

LINDISFARNE PRIORY

The site of one of the most important early centres of Christianity in Anglo-Saxon England. St Cuthbert converted pagan Northumbria, and miracles occurring at his shrine established this 11th century priory as a major pilgrimage centre. The evocative ruins, with the decorated 'rainbow' arch curving dramatically across the nave of the church, are still the destination of pilgrims today. The story of Lindisfarne is told in an exhibition which gives an impression of life for the monks, including a reconstruction of a monk's cell.

All year (subject to tide times). £1.80/£1.40/90p.

(028989) 200

On Holy Island, which can be reached at low tide across a causeway. Tide tables are posted at each end of the causeway. (OS Map 75; ref NU 126418). Bus: *Northumbria 477 from Berwick-upon-Tweed (passes close BR Berwick-upon-Tweed). Times vary with tides (Tel: 0289 307283).* Station: *Berwick-upon-Tweed 14m via causeway.*

NORHAM CASTLE

Set on a promontory in a curve of the River Tweed, this was one of the strongest of the border castles, built c.1160.

⊙ *All year. £1.10/85p/55p.*

⮜ *(excluding keep)*

✆ *(028982) 329*

➲ *Norham village, 6½m SW of Berwick-upon-Tweed on minor road off B6470 (from A698). (OS Map 75; ref NT 907476). Bus: Swan/ Northumbria/Lowland 23 BR Berwick-upon-Tweed — Kelso (Tel: 0289 306436 & 307461). Station: Berwick-upon-Tweed 7½m.*

Norham Castle

Lindisfarne Priory

PRUDHOE CASTLE

The extensive remains of this 12th century castle include a gatehouse, curtain wall and keep. There is much to see, including a video about the castles of Northumbria.

⊙ *All year. £1.50/£1.10/75p.*

✆ *(0661) 833459*

➲ *In Prudhoe, on minor road off A695. (OS Map 88; ref NZ 092634). Bus: From surrounding areas (Tel: 091-232 4211). Station: Prudhoe ¼m.*

Prudhoe Castle

WARKWORTH CASTLE AND HERMITAGE

The great towering keep of this 15th century castle dominates the town and River Coquet. Just upstream by boat is a curious hermitage cut from the rock.

⊙ *Castle: All year. £1.10/85p/55p. Hermitage: Summer season, weekends only (access by boat) 75p/55p/40p.*

⮜ *(at castle) (castle, excluding keep)*

✆ *(0665) 711423*

➲ *7½m S of Alnwick on A1068. (OS Map 81; Castle ref NU 247057, Hermitage ref NU 242060). Bus: Northumbria X18 Newcastle-Alnwick (Tel: 091-232 4211). Station: Alnmouth 3½m.*

Warkworth Castle

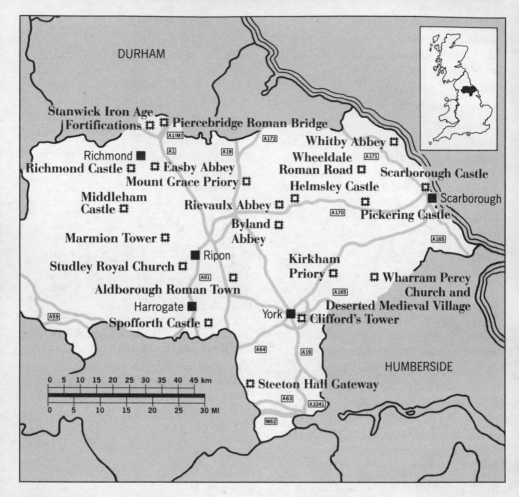

DURHAM

Stanwick Iron Age
Fortifications ✛ ✛ Piercebridge Roman Bridge
A1(M)
A1   A172
Richmond ■   A19   Whitby Abbey ✛
Richmond Castle ✛   ✛ Easby Abbey   Wheeldale   A171
Mount Grace Priory ✛   Roman Road ✛   Scarborough Castle
Middleham   Helmsley Castle   ✛
Castle ✛   Rievaulx Abbey ✛   ✛   Scarborough ■ Scarborough
A170   Pickering Castle
Byland ✛
Marmion Tower ✛   Abbey   A165
■ Ripon
Studley Royal Church ✛   Kirkham
A61   ✛   Priory ✛   ✛ Wharram Percy
Aldborough Roman Town   A165   Church and
Harrogate ■   Deserted Medieval Village
Spofforth Castle ✛   York ■ ✛ Clifford's Tower
A59
A64   A19
HUMBERSIDE
0 5 10 15 20 25 30 35 40 45 km
✛ Steeton Hall Gateway
0   5   10   15   20   25   30 MI   A63
A1041
M62

ORTH YORKSHIRE HAS BOTH some of the finest monuments and
some of the most beautiful scenery in Britain.

The scenery provides some spectacular backdrops to the
monuments. Middleham Castle, childhood home of Richard III, stands in
beautiful Wensleydale. A few miles north you will find Richmond Castle and
Easby Abbey.

The idyllic setting of Mount Grace Priory could be your next stop, en route
to Rievaulx Abbey, the most spectacular monastic ruin in the England. Nearby
are Helmsley Castle and Byland Abbey.

After driving to Pickering Castle two routes offer themselves. One is the
North Yorkshire Moors Railway, which runs through stunning scenery and on to
Whitby; the other is to travel via Scarborough and its large 12th century castle.

ALDBOROUGH ROMAN TOWN 🔥

Once the principal town of the Brigantes, the largest tribe in Roman Britain. The remains include parts of the Roman town wall and two mosaic pavements. A museum displays finds from the site.

🕐 *Summer season. £1.10/85p/55p. Oct-Mar grounds only, admission free.*

🚹 *(Summer only)* 🛍 ⊗ 🅿

✆ *(0423) 322768*

➲ *¾m SE of Boroughbridge, on minor road off B6265. (OS Map 99; ref SE 405667). Bus: United 142 BR York-Ripon (Tel: 0325 468771).*

Aldborough Roman Town

BYLAND ABBEY 🐟

A hauntingly beautiful ruin, set in peaceful meadows in the shadow of the Hambleton Hills. It illustrates later developments of Cistercian churches, including a beautiful floor of mosaic tiles.

🕐 *All year. £1.10/85p/55p.*

🅿 🚹 ♿ *(including 🚹)* 🛍 🅿 🅿

✆ *(03476) 614*

➲ *2m S of A170 between Thirsk and Helmsley, near Coxwold village. (OS Map 100; ref SE 549789).*

CLIFFORD'S TOWER, YORK 🏰

A 13th century tower on one of two mottes thrown up by William the Conqueror to hold York. There are panoramic views of the city from the top of the tower.

🕐 *All year, plus Mondays in Winter. £1.10/85p/55p.*

🅿 *(city council)* ⊗

✆ *(0904) 646940*

➲ *In Castle St (OS Map 105; ref SE 605515). Bus: From surrounding areas (Tel: 0904 624161). Station: York 1m.*

Clifford's Tower

Byland Abbey

NORTH YORKSHIRE

EASBY ABBEY 🏛

Substantial remains of the medieval abbey buildings stand in a beautiful setting by the River Swale near Richmond.

🕐 *All year.*

🅿 🍴 ⊛

➡ *1m SE of Richmond off B6271. (OS Map 92; ref NZ 185003). Bus: United 27/A/B, 28/ A BR Darlington-Richmond thence 1½m (Tel: 0325 468771).*

Easby Abbey

🎟 HELMSLEY CASTLE 🏰

Close to the market square, with a view of the town, is this 12th century castle. Spectacular earthworks surround a great ruined keep dating from the Norman Conquest. There is an exhibition and tableau on the history of the castle.

🕐 *All year. £1.50/£1.10/75p.*

🅿 *(large car park north of castle)* ⊛

☎ *(0439) 70442*

➡ *Near town centre. (OS Map 100; ref SE 611836). Bus: Scarborough & District 128 from BR Scarborough (Tel: 0723 375463); Yorkshire Coastliner 94 from BR Malton (Tel: 0653 692556).*

Helmsley Castle

KIRKHAM PRIORY 🏛

The ruins of this Augustinian priory, including a magnificent carved gatehouse, are set in a peaceful and secluded valley by the River Derwent.

🕐 *All year. £1.10/85p/55p.*

🅿 ♿ 🍴 ⊛

☎ *(065381) 768*

➡ *5m SW of Malton on minor road off A64. (OS Map 100; ref SE 735657). Bus: Yorkshire Coastliner 840/3 Leeds-Scarborough (pass BR York and Malton) to within ¾m (Tel: 0653 692556). Station: Malton 6m.*

Kirkham Priory

MARMION TOWER 🏰

A medieval gatehouse, which once guarded a ferry crossing, with a fine oriel window.

🕐 *All year.*

⊛

➡ *N of Ripon on A6108 in West Tanfield. (OS Map 99; ref SE 267787). Station: Thirsk 10m.*

112

MIDDLEHAM CASTLE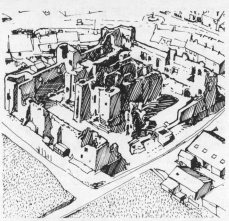

This childhood home of Richard III stands controlling the river that winds through Wensleydale. There is a massive 12th century keep standing within later fortifications.

⊕ *All year. £1.10/85p/55p.*

🛆 🏭 ⊛

☎ *(0969) 23899*

➲ *At Middleham, 2m S of Leyburn on A6108. (OS Map 99; ref SE 128875).*

Middleham Castle

MOUNT GRACE PRIORY 🏠

The only well preserved Carthusian monastery in England, founded in 1398 and beautifully situated in attractive woodland. Each of the monks had his own two-storey cell, one of which has been fully restored and now contains hand carved replica cabinets, beds and chests. There are also extensive remains of the cloister, church and outer court.

⊕ *All year. £1.80/£1.40/90p.*

🚻 🅿 ♿ 🏭 ⊛

☎ *(0609) 83494*

➲ *7m NE of Northallerton on A19 near Ingleby Arncliffe. (OS Map 99; ref SE 453982). Bus: United/Tees & District 90/A Northallerton-Middlesbrough (pass close BR Northallerton) to within ½m (Tel: 0642 210131). Station: Northallerton 6m.*

PICKERING CASTLE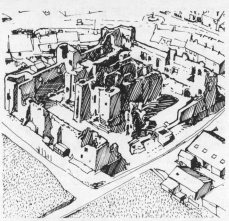

A splendid motte and bailey castle, once a royal ranch. It is well preserved, with much of the original walls, towers and keep, and there are spectacular views over the surrounding countryside.

⊕ *All year. £1.50/£1.10/75p.*

🅿 ♿ *(except motte)* 🏭 ⊛ 📋 🛆

☎ *(0751) 74989*

➲ *In Pickering, 15m SW of Scarborough. (OS Map 100; ref SE 800845). Bus: Yorkshire Coastliner 840/2 from BR Malton (Tel: 0653 692556); Scarborough & District 128 from BR Scarborough (Tel: 0723 37563). Station: Malton 9m; Pickering (N York Moors Rly) ¼m.*

Mount Grace Priory

Pickering Castle

113

PIERCEBRIDGE ROMAN BRIDGE

Recently discovered remains of the piers and abutment of a Roman timber bridge across the River Tees.

⊙ *Any reasonable time.*

⊛

➲ *At Piercebridge, 4m W of Darlington on B6275. (OS Map 93; ref NZ 214154). Bus: United 75/A BR Darlington-Barnard Castle (Tel: 0325 468771). Station: Darlington 5m.*

RIEVAULX ABBEY

In a deeply wooded valley by the River Rye you can see some of the most spectacular monastic ruins in England, dating from the 12th century. The church has the earliest large Cistercian nave in Britain. A fascinating exhibition shows how successfully the Cistercians at Rievaulx ran their many businesses and explains the part played by Abbot Ailred, who ruled for twenty years.

⊙ *All year. £1.80/£1.40/90p*

📄 🛗 🚻 🅿 🎧 ♿ 🛍 🗋 ⊛

✆ *(04396) 228*

➲ *2¼m W of Helmsley on minor road off B1257. (OS Map 100; ref SE 577849). Bus: YorkTour Heritage Bus from BR York (Tel: 0904 645151); Tees & District 294 from Middlesbrough (passes close BR Middlesbrough), Fri only (Tel: 0642 21013); otherwise Scarborough & District 128 Scarborough-Helmsley to within 3m (Tel: 0723 375463).*

Rievaulx Abbey

RICHMOND CASTLE

A splendid medieval fortress, with a fine 12th century keep and 11th century remains of the curtain wall and domestic buildings. From the battlements you can see nearby Easby Abbey.

⊙ *All year. £1.50/£1.10/75p.*

🚻 ♿ 🛍 🗋 ⊛

✆ *(0748) 822493*

➲ *In Richmond. (OS Map 92; ref NZ 174006). Bus: United 27/A/B, 28/A BR Darlington-Richmond (Tel: 0325 468771).*

Richmond Castle

SCARBOROUGH CASTLE

From the walls of this enormous 12th century castle you will have spectacular coastal views. The buttressed castle walls stretch out along the cliff edge and the remains of the great rectangular stone keep still stand to over three storeys high. There is also the site of a 4th century Roman signal station. The castle was frequently attacked, but despite being blasted by cannons of the Civil War and bombarded from the sea during World War I, it is still a spectacular place to visit.

⊙ *All year. £1.50/£1.10/75p.*

🚻 🎧 ♿ *(except keep)* 🛍 🗋 ⊛

✆ *(0723) 372451*

➲ *Castle Rd, E of town centre. (OS Map 101; ref TA 050893). Bus: From surrounding areas (Tel: 0723 375463). Station: Scarborough 1m.*

SPOFFORTH CASTLE ⌂

This manor house has some fascinating features including an undercroft built into the rock. It was once owned by the Percy family.

☉ *All year.*

⊛

➡ *3½m SE of Harrogate, on minor road off A661 at Spofforth. (OS Map 104; ref SE 360511). Bus: Harrogate & District 78/A, 79 Harrogate-York (Tel: 0423 566061). Station: Pannal 4m.*

STANWICK IRON AGE FORTIFICATIONS ⌂

The excavated section of the ditch, cut into the rock, and the rampart of vast earthworks covers some 850 acres. Once the tribal stronghold of the Brigantes.

☉ *Any reasonable time.*

⊛

➡ *9m W of Darlington on B6275. (OS Map 92; ref NZ 179112). Station: Darlington 10m.*

Scarborough Castle

STEETON HALL GATEWAY ⌂

A fine example of a small, well preserved 14th century gatehouse.

☉ *Any reasonable time. Key available from Area Office.*

& ⊛

✆ *(0904) 658626*

➡ *4m NE of Castleford, on minor road off A162 at South Milford. (OS Map 105; ref SE 484314). Station: South Milford 1m.*

STUDLEY ROYAL: ST MARY'S CHURCH ⌂

A magnificent Victorian church, designed by William Burges in the 1870's, with a highly decorated interior. Coloured marble, stained glass, gilded and painted figures and a splendid organ still remain in their original glory.

☉ *Summer season, daily 1-5pm. The Studley Royal estate, including Fountains Abbey, is managed by the National Trust. Estate tel. (0765) 620333.*

🅿 *(NT — charge payable)* & ⊛

➡ *2½m W of Ripon off B6265, in grounds of Studley Royal estate. (OS Map 99; ref SE 278703). Bus: YorkTour Heritage Bus from BR York (Tel: 0904 645151); United 145 from Ripon (with connections from BR Harrogate), Thurs, Sat only (Tel: 0325 468771); Dalesbus 806 from Leeds, Summer only (passes close BR Harrogate) (Tel: 0423 566061).*

WHEELDALE ROMAN ROAD ⌂

This mile long stretch of Roman road, still with its hardcore and drainage ditches, runs across isolated moorland.

☉ *Any reasonable time.*

⊛

➡ *S of Goathland, W of A169, 7m S of Whitby. (OS Map 94; ref SE 805975). Station: Goathland (N York Moors Rly) 4m.*

WHITBY ABBEY 🏛

This is an ancient holy place, once a burial-place of kings and the inspiration for saints. A religious community was first established at Whitby in 657 by Abbess Hilda and was the home of Caedmon, the first English poet. The remains we can see today are of a Benedictine church built in the 13th and 14th centuries, and include a magnificent three-tiered choir and north transept. It is perched high above the picturesque harbour town of Whitby.

🕐 *All year. £1.10/85p/55p.*

🚻 🅿 *(both local council)* 🎫 🛈 🌐 🗋

✆ *(0947) 603568*

➲ *On cliff top E of Whitby town centre. (OS Map 94; ref NZ 904115).* Bus: *From surrounding areas (Tel: 0947 602146).* Station: *Whitby ½m.*

Whitby Abbey

WHARRAM PERCY CHURCH AND DESERTED MEDIEVAL VILLAGE 🏛

One of over 3,000 deserted villages to have been identified from faint outlines of walls and foundations. The remains of the medieval church still stand and excavated houses can also be seen.

🕐 *Any reasonable time. Guided tours of annual excavations in July. Contact Regional Office for details 091-261 1585.*

🅿 *(at Bella Farm, ¾m walk to site)* 🎫 🌐

➲ *6m SE of Malton, on minor road from B1248 ½m S of Wharram le Street (OS Map 100; ref SE 859645).* Station: *Malton 8m.*

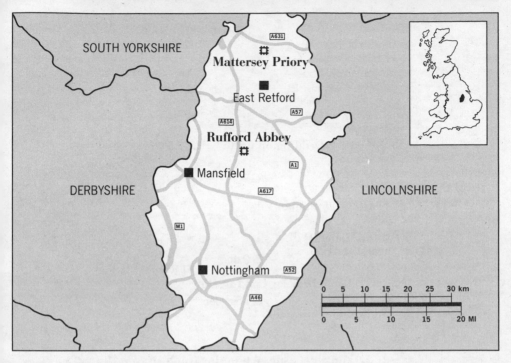

S ANDWICHED BETWEEN DERBYSHIRE and Lincolnshire is the
county of Nottinghamshire. From the city of Nottingham at its southern
end, running north through the heart of the county are the remains of
the once massive Sherwood Forest, which played so significant a part in the
Robin Hood legend.

MATTERSEY PRIORY ⚓

Remains of a small Gilbertine monastery
founded in 1185, set in farmland and
almost encircled by the River Idle.

🕐 *Any reasonable time.*

🈂️

➲ *1m E of Mattersey off B6045, 7m N of East
Retford (OS Map 112; ref SK 704896).*
Station: *Retford 7m.*

RUFFORD ABBEY ⚓

A 12th century Cistercian abbey once
largely concealed by a 17th century
country house. Its demolition in the
1950's has revealed the remains of the lay
brothers' quarters. Rufford Country Park
has attractive grounds and facilities.

🕐 *All year (closes 5pm in Summer).*

🚻 🅿 🍴 🗋 ♿ ⊗ *craft centre*

✆ *(0623) 823148*

➲ *2m S of Ollerton off A614 (OS Map 120;
ref SK 645646).* Bus: *East Midland 33
Nottingham-Worksop, 36 Nottingham-
Doncaster (Tel: 0602 240000).*

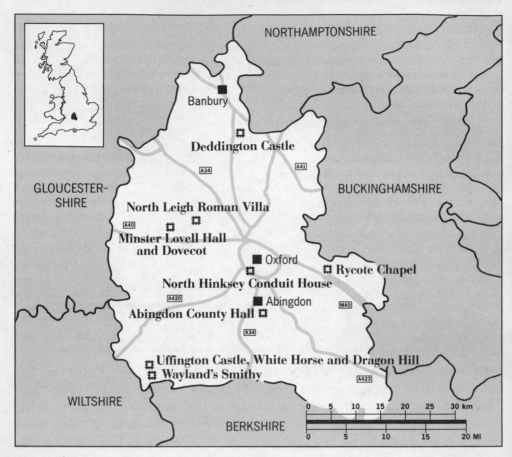

NORTHAMPTONSHIRE

Banbury

☒ Deddington Castle

A34   A41

GLOUCESTER-
SHIRE

BUCKINGHAMSHIRE

North Leigh Roman Villa

A40

Minster Lovell Hall
and Dovecot

■ Oxford

☒ Rycote Chapel

North Hinksey Conduit House

A420

■ Abingdon

M40

Abingdon County Hall

A34

☒ Uffington Castle, White Horse and Dragon Hill
☒ Wayland's Smithy

A423

WILTSHIRE

0 5 10 15 20 25 30 km

0   5   10   15   20 MI

BERKSHIRE

O XFORDSHIRE BEGINS WITH the Cotswolds on its western side,
running down into the Thames Valley, before rising again on the eastern
side towards the Chiltern escarpment.

In the north of the county the land is gentle and undulating, to the south
there is chalk — and the magnificent White Horse Hill, cut into the turf at
Uffington, and large Iron Age camp.

Oxfordshire is noted for its churches, many well known. Others, like the
15th century Rycote Chapel remain largely undiscovered.

There are many other hidden-away places to find: North Leigh Roman
Villa, Minster Lovell Hall and Dovecote, and Waylands's Smithy — a prehistoric
burial chamber.

But the centre of the county is Oxford. Its beauty and dignity survive in the
form of its illustrious university — its colleges turned in on themselves, reflecting
in their quadrangles a far quieter age.

ABINGDON COUNTY HALL

A grand centrepiece for the market place at Abingdon, this 17th century public building was built to house the Assize Courts and was constructed over an open market hall. It now houses a museum depicting many aspects of Abingdon.

⏱ *Museum open 1 Apr-31 Oct 1-5pm, 1 Nov-31 Mar 1-4pm. Closed Mon & Bank Holidays.*

🚫 ⑩

➡ *In Abingdon, 7m S of Oxford in Market Place (OS Map 164; ref SU 497971). Bus: Oxford 35-7, Oxford Minibus 30/A from Oxford (pass BR Radley) (Tel: 0865 711312 & 727000). Station: Radley 2½m.*

DEDDINGTON CASTLE 🏰

Extensive earthworks concealing the remains of a 12th century castle which was ruined as early as the 14th century.

⏱ *Any reasonable time.*

🚫

➡ *S of B4031 on E side of Deddington, 17m N of Oxford on A423 (OS Map 151; SP 471316). Bus: Midland Red X59 Oxford-Banbury to within ½m (Tel: 0295 262368). Station: King's Sutton 5m.*

North Leigh Roman Villa

MINSTER LOVELL HALL AND DOVECOTE 🏰

The handsome ruins of Lord Lovell's 15th century manor house stand in a lovely setting on the banks of the River Windrush. A delightful medieval dovecote with nesting boxes complete is nearby.

⏱ *Summer season. 95p/70p/50p.*

🅿 🚫

☎ *(0993) 775315*

➡ *Adjacent to Minster Lovell church, 3m W of Witney off A40 (OS Map 164; ref SP 324114). Bus: Swanbrook Oxford-Tewkesbury (Tel: 0242 574444). Station: Charlbury 7m.*

Minster Lovell Hall

NORTH LEIGH ROMAN VILLA 🏛

In a pleasant wooded valley, you will find the remains of this large and well built Roman courtyard villa. The most important feature is an almost complete mosaic tile floor, intricately patterned in reds and browns.

⏱ *Any reasonable time. Pedestrian access only from main road (600yds).*

🚫

➡ *2m N of North Leigh, 9m W of Oxford off A4095 (OS Map 164; ref SP 397154).*

NORTH HINKSEY CONDUIT HOUSE

The roofed reservoir for Oxford's first water mains, built in the early 17th century. Water collected here was piped to Carfax conduit.

⊕ *Any reasonable time (exterior only).*

⊛

➡ *In North Hinksey off A34, 2½m W of Oxford (OS Map 164; ref SP 494054). Bus: Frequent from Oxford (Tel: 0865 727000 & 711312). Station: Oxford 2m.*

RYCOTE CHAPEL ⚑

This lovely and peaceful 15th century chapel, with exquisitely carved and painted woodwork, has many intriguing features, including two roofed pews and a musicians' gallery.

⊕ *Keykeeper. Tel. (06723) 370 for details.*

🅿 ♿ *(assistance required)* ⊛

➡ *3m SW of Thame off A329 (OS Map 165; ref SP 667046). Bus: Oxford/Aylesbury Bus/ Motts 260, 280, X80 Oxford-Aylesbury (pass BR Haddenham & Thame Parkway) to within ¼m (Tel: 0296 382000). Station: Haddenham & Thame Parkway 5m.*

UFFINGTON CASTLE, WHITE HORSE AND DRAGON HILL ⚑

A group of sites lying along The Ridgeway, an old prehistoric route. There is a large Iron Age camp enclosed within ramparts, a natural mound known as Dragon Hill and the White Horse, cut from turf to reveal chalk.

⊕ *Any reasonable time.*

🅿 ⊛

➡ *S of B4507, 7m W of Wantage (OS Map 174; ref SU 301866).*

WAYLAND'S SMITHY ⚑

An unusual Neolithic burial site where two grave types lie one upon the other.

⊕ *Any reasonable time.*

⊛

➡ *On the Ridgeway ¾m NE of B4000 Ashbury-Lambourn road. (OS Map 174; ref SU 281854).*

Rycote Chapel

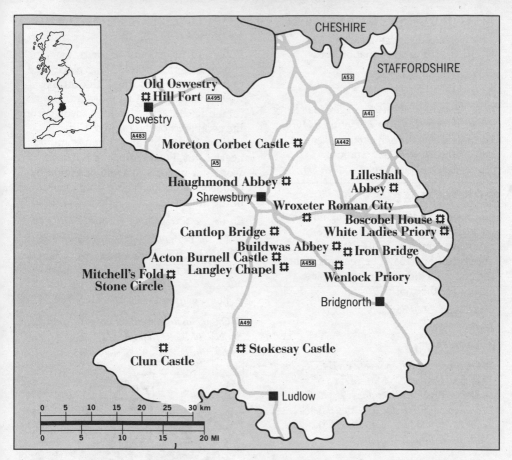

CHESHIRE

STAFFORDSHIRE

Old Oswestry
⚏ **Hill Fort** A495
Oswestry

Moreton Corbet Castle ⚏

Haughmond Abbey ⚏

Lilleshall Abbey ⚏

Shrewsbury ■

Wroxeter Roman City
⚏

Boscobel House ⚏

Cantlop Bridge ⚏

White Ladies Priory ⚏

Buildwas Abbey ⚏
⚏ **Iron Bridge**

Acton Burnell Castle ⚏

Langley Chapel ⚏

Mitchell's Fold ⚏
Stone Circle

Wenlock Priory

Bridgnorth ■

⚏
Clun Castle

⚏ **Stokesay Castle**

■ Ludlow

0 5 10 15 20 25 30 km

0 5 10 15 20 MI

WITH PREHISTORIC STONE CIRCLES, Iron Age hill forts, medieval abbeys, castles, manor houses and monuments of the industrial revolution, Shropshire encapsulates a complete history of Britain.

One of the finest and most beautiful buildings in Shropshire is Stokesay Castle which is a largely unaltered 13th century fortified manor house.

Many fine churches and abbeys remain from the 12th and 13th centuries. Among them is Buildwas Abbey which is virtually complete apart from its roof. Another abbey at Lilleshall is an extensive ruin, and includes an aisleless nave. There are also remains at Wenlock Priory of a 13th century Cluniac priory.

To the east is Boscobel House — a timber framed hunting lodge, in which Charles II hid in a nearby oak tree after the Battle of Worcester in 1651.

As a final contrast, Shropshire also has a fine industrial heritage. Ironbridge takes its name from the world's first iron bridge, probably Britain's best-known industrial monument.

ACTON BURNELL CASTLE 🏰

The warm red sandstone shell of a fortified 13th century manor house.

🕐 *Any reasonable time.*

 ♿ ⊗

➲ *In Acton Burnell, on unclassified road 8m S of Shrewsbury (OS Map 126; ref SJ 534019).* Bus: *Boultons from Shrewsbury, Tues, Sat only (Tel: 0345 056 785).* Station: *Shrewsbury or Church Stretton, both 8m.*

BUILDWAS ABBEY 🏛

Set beside the River Severn, against a backdrop of wooded grounds, are extensive remains of this Cistercian abbey built in 1135. The remains include the church which is almost complete except for the roof.

🕐 *All year. £1.10/85p/55p.*

♿ ⊗

📞 *(0952) 433274*

➲ *On S bank of River Severn on B4378, 2m W of Iron Bridge (OS Map 127; ref SJ 642044).* Bus: *Williamsons X96 Birmingham-Shrewsbury (passes close BR Telford Central) (Tel: 0345 056 785).* Station: *Telford Central 6m.*

Buildwas Abbey

BOSCOBEL HOUSE AND THE ROYAL OAK 🏠 ✿

Fully refurnished and restored, the panelled rooms, secret hiding places and pretty gardens lend this 17th century timber-framed hunting lodge a truly romantic character. Its fame springs from the escapades of the fugitive King Charles II who hid in the house and the nearby Royal Oak, after the Battle of Worcester in 1651, to avoid detection by Cromwell's troops. There is an exhibition in the house.

🕐 *All year (except Jan). £2.80/£2.10/£1.40.*

📋 🛈 🚻 🅿 🍴 *(1 April-30 Sept, open Tues-Sun; 1 Oct-31 Dec, open Suns only; 1 Feb-31 March, open weekends only.)* ♿ *(gardens only)* 🖴 ⊗

📞 *(0902) 850244*

➲ *On unclassified road between A41 and A5, 8m NW of Wolverhampton (OS Map 127; ref SJ 837083).* Station: *Cosford 3m.*

Boscobel House

CANTLOP BRIDGE ⌒

Single-span cast-iron road bridge over the Cound Brook, designed by the great engineer Thomas Telford.

🕐 *Any reasonable time.*

⊗

➲ *¾m SW of Berrington on unclassified road off A458 (OS Map 126; ref SJ 517062).* Station: *Shrewsbury 5m.*

CLUN CASTLE 🏰

The remains of the four storey keep and other buildings of this border castle are set in outstandingly beautiful countryside. Built by the de Say family in the 11th century, the castle eventually passed into the ownership of the Dukes of Norfolk.

🕐 *Any reasonable time.*

🌐 🎫

➤ *In Clun, off A488, 18m W of Ludlow. (OS Map 137; ref SO 299809).* Bus: *Midland Red West 743-5 from Ludlow (pass close BR Ludlow) (Tel: 0345 212 555).* Station: *Hopton Heath 6½m; Knighton 6½m.*

HAUGHMOND ABBEY 🏛

Set in pleasant wooded countryside, there are extensive remains of this 12th century Augustinian abbey, including the Chapter House, which retains its late medieval timber ceiling, and some fine medieval sculpture.

🕐 *All year. £1.10/85p/55p.*

🅿 ♿ 🌐

☎ *(074377) 661*

➤ *3m NE of Shrewsbury off B5062 (OS Map 126; ref SJ 542152).* Bus: *Shearings from Shrewsbury (Tel: 0345 056 785).* Station: *Shrewsbury 3½m.*

IRON BRIDGE 🌉

The world's first iron bridge and Britain's best-known industrial monument. Cast in Coalbrookdale by local ironmaster Abraham Darby, it was erected across the River Severn in 1779.

🕐 *Any reasonable time.*

🌐

➤ *In Ironbridge, adjacent to A4169 (OS Map 127; ref SJ 672034).* Bus: *Frequent from Telford (pass close BR Telford Central or Wellington Telford West) (Tel: 0345 056 785).* Station: *Telford Central 5m.*

LANGLEY CHAPEL 🏛

A delightful medieval chapel, standing alone in a field, with a complete set of early 17th century wooden fittings and furniture.

🕐 *All year.*

🌐

☎ *Area Office: (0902) 765105*

➤ *1½m S of Acton Burnell, on unclassified road off A49 9½m S of Shrewsbury (OS Map 126; ref SJ 538001).* Bus: *Boultons from Shrewsbury, Tues, Sat only, to within 1½m (Tel: 0345 056 785).* Station: *Shrewsbury 7½m.*

Haughmond Abbey

LILLESHALL ABBEY

Extensive and evocative ruins of an abbey of Augustinian canons, including remains of the 12th and 13th century church and the cloister buildings, surrounded by green lawns and ancient yew trees.

⏱ *Any reasonable time.*

🌐

➡ *On unclassified road off A518, 4m N of Oakengates (OS Map 127; ref SJ 738142). Bus: Midland Red North 81/2 Telford-Newport (pass close BR Telford Central) to within 1m (Tel: 0345 056 785). Station: Oakengates 4½m.*

MITCHELL'S FOLD STONE CIRCLE

An air of mystery surrounds this Bronze Age stone circle, set on dramatic moorland and consisting of some 30 stones of which 15 are visible.

⏱ *Any reasonable time.*

🌐

➡ *16m SW of Shrewsbury W of A488 (OS Map 137; ref SO 306984). Bus: Minsterley, Horrocks Shrewsbury-Bishop's Castle (pass close BR Shrewsbury) to within 1m (Tel: 0345 056 785). Station: Welshpool 10m.*

MORETON CORBET CASTLE

A ruined medieval castle with the substantial remains of a splendid Elizabethan mansion, captured in 1644 from Charles I's supporters by Parliamentary forces.

⏱ *Any reasonable time.*

🅿 ♿ 🌐

➡ *In Moreton Corbet off B5063, 7m NE of Shrewsbury (OS Map 126; ref SJ 562232). Bus: Midland Red North/PMT X64 Shrewsbury-Hanley (passes close BR Shrewsbury & Stoke-on-Trent) (Tel: 0345 056 785). Station: Yorton 4m.*

Lilleshall Abbey

OLD OSWESTRY HILL FORT

An impressive Iron Age fort of 68 acres defended by a series of five ramparts with an elaborate western entrance and unusual earthwork cisterns.

⏱ *Any reasonable time.*

🌐

➡ *1m N of Oswestry, accessible from unclassified road off A483 (OS Map 126; ref SJ 295310). Bus: Crosville Wales 2, D53, D63 from BR Gobowen (Tel: 0345 056 785). Station: Gobowen 2m.*

STOKESAY CASTLE

A rare and wonderfully preserved example of a 13th century fortified manor house situated in peaceful countryside. The castle now stands in a picturesque group with its own splendid timber-framed Jacobean gatehouse and the parish church.

⏱ *6 Mar-31 Oct, daily except Tues 10am-6pm (5pm in Mar & Oct); 1-30 Nov open weekends only, 10am-4pm. Parties during the week by arrangement. £2/£2/£1 (no reduction for OAPs, students or unemployed).*

👫 🅿 ♿ *(gardens & great hall only)* 🌐

📞 *(0588) 672544*

➡ *1m S of Craven Arms off A49 (OS Map 137; ref SO 436817). Bus: Midland Red West 435 Shrewsbury-Ludlow (Tel: 0345 212 555). Station: Craven Arms 1m.*

WENLOCK PRIORY 🏛

The ruins of a large Cluniac priory in an attractive garden setting featuring delightful topiary. There are substantial remains of the early 13th century church and Norman chapter house.

⊙ *All year. £1.50/£1.10/75p.*

🅿 🎧 ⊛

✆ *(0952) 727466*

➲ *In Much Wenlock (OS Map 127; ref SJ 625001). Bus: Midland Red West 436/7 Shrewsbury-Bridgnorth (pass close BR Shrewsbury) (Tel: 0345 056 785). Station: Ironbridge (Summer Sundays only) 5m; Telford Central 9m.*

Wenlock Priory

Stokesay Castle

WHITE LADIES PRIORY 🏛

The ruins of the late 12th century church of a small priory of Augustinian canonesses, converted to a house after the Dissolution. Charles II hid here and in nearby woods in 1651 before moving to Boscobel.

⊙ *Any reasonable time.*

⊛

➲ *1m SW of Boscobel House off unclassified road between A41 and A5, 8m NW of Wolverhampton (OS Map 127; ref SJ 826076). Station: Cosford 2½m.*

WROXETER ROMAN CITY 🪖

The excavated centre of the fourth largest city in Roman Britain, with impressive remains of the 2nd century municipal baths. The museum has finds from the town and earlier legionary fortress.

⊙ *All year. £1.50/£1.10/75p.*

📗 🛍 🅿 ♿ ⊛ 🅿 🚻

✆ *(074375) 330*

➲ *At Wroxeter, 5m E of Shrewsbury 1m S of A5 (OS Map 126; ref SJ 568088). Bus: Williamson X96 Birmingham-Shrewsbury (passes close BR Telford Central) (Tel: 0345 056 785). Station: Shrewsbury 5½m; Wellington Telford West 6m.*

Wroxeter Roman City

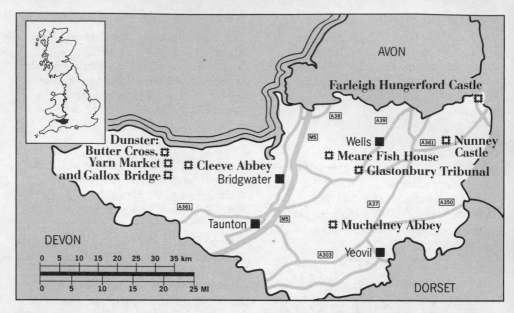

S OMERSET HAS PROVIDED a home to communities since the earliest times. Prehistoric hunters sheltered in the Mendip Hills, and Saxons grazed their cattle on its pastures.

Somerset still has a soft rural landscape, now dotted with pretty houses, and laced with quiet winding lanes. A dramatic backdrop to this serenity is formed by the Quantock Hills.

Water also plays an element in the landscape. The drained fenland of the Somerset Levels have been reclaimed from the sea and the bog over thousands of years.

Lake villages were developed as early as the Iron Age. From the village at Meare, the 14th century Fish House supplied the abbey at nearby Glastonbury.

Apart from Glastonbury, other important ecclesiastical ruins can be found at the 10th century Muchelney Abbey, and Cistercian Cleeve Abbey.

CLEEVE ABBEY 🏛

There are few monastic sites where you will see such a complete set of cloister buildings, including the refectory with its magnificent timber roof. Built in the 13th century, this Cistercian abbey was saved from destruction at the Dissolution by being turned into a house and then a farm.

🕐 All year. £1.50/£1.10/75p.

🚻 🅿 ☢ ♿ (grounds & ground floor only) 📋 🗋 🛍

☎ (0984) 40377

➜ In Washford, ¼m S of A39 (OS Map 181; ref ST 047407). Bus: Southern National 28/C BR Taunton-Minehead, also 38 from Minehead (Tel: 0823 272033). Station: Washford (W Somerset Rly) ½m.

DUNSTER: BUTTER CROSS

A medieval stone cross that now stands away from the centre of this delightful village but possibly once stood in the high street.

⊕ *Any reasonable time.*

⊛

➡ *Beside the minor road to Alcombe, 400yds NW of Dunster parish church (OS Map 181; ref SS 988439). Bus: Southern National 28/C BR Taunton-Minehead, also 38/9 from Minehead to within ½m (Tel: 0823 272033). Station: Dunster (W Somerset Rly) 1m.*

DUNSTER: GALLOX BRIDGE

A stone packhorse bridge with two ribbed arches which spans the old mill stream in a picture-book setting.

⊕ *Any reasonable time.*

& ⊛

➡ *Off A396 at S end of Dunster (OS Map 181; ref SS 990432). Bus: Southern National 28/C BR Taunton-Minehead, also 38/9 from Minehead to within ⅛m (Tel: 0823 272033). Station: Dunster (W Somerset Rly) ¾m.*

Cleeve Abbey

DUNSTER: YARN MARKET

Dominating the centre of this ancient village, this 17th century octagonal market hall was used for the sale of locally woven cloth.

⊕ *Any reasonable time.*

& ⊛

➡ *In Dunster High St (OS Map 181; ref SS 992437). Bus: Southern National 28/C BR Taunton-Minehead, also 38/9 from Minehead to within ¼m (Tel: 0823 272033). Station: Dunster (W Somerset Rly) ½m.*

ᴎ FARLEIGH HUNGERFORD CASTLE ᴍ

Extensive ruins of a 14th century castle with a splendid chapel containing wall paintings, stained glass and the fine tomb of Sir Thomas Hungerford, builder of the castle.

⊕ *All year. £1.10/85p/55p.*

ⁱⁱⁱ ᴾ ⊗ & *(exterior only).*

𝑐 *(0225) 754026*

➡ *In Farleigh Hungerford 3½m W of Trowbridge on A366 (OS Map 173; ref ST 801577). Bus: Badgerline X3 Bristol-BR Frome (passes BR Bath Spa) to within 1m (Tel: 0272 297979). Station: Avoncliff 2m; Trowbridge 3½m.*

Farleigh Hungerford Castle

GLASTONBURY TRIBUNAL 🏛

A well preserved medieval town house, reputedly once used as the courthouse of Glastonbury Abbey and converted to a private dwelling after the Dissolution. The house now incorporates the museum of the Glastonbury Antiquarian Society.

🕐 *All year. £1.10/85p/55p.*

⊗ ♿ *(ground floor only — 2 steps)* 🅼

📞 *(0458) 32949*

➡ *In Glastonbury High St (OS Map 182; ref ST 499390). Bus: Badgerline 376, 677, Southern National 29/A. BR Bristol Temple Meads-Street (Tel: 0823 255696).*

Glastonbury Tribunal

MEARE FISH HOUSE 🏛

The home of the chief fisherman to Glastonbury Abbey, this simple well preserved stone dwelling now stands in the middle of a field, the fishponds having dried up long ago.

🕐 *Any reasonable time. Key from Manor House farm.*

⊗

➡ *In Meare village on B3151 (OS Map 182; ref ST 458418).*

MUCHELNEY ABBEY 🏛

Well preserved remains of the cloisters, with windows carved in golden stone, and abbot's lodging of this Benedictine abbey, which survived by being used as a farmhouse after the Dissolution.

🕐 *Summer season. £1.10/85p/55p.*

♿ 🅿 ⊗ ♿ *(grounds and part of ground floor only).*

📞 *(0458) 250664*

➡ *In Muchelney 2m S of Langport (OS Map 193; ref ST 428248). Bus: Southern National 54 Taunton-Yeovil (passes close BR Taunton) to within 1m (Tel: 0823 272033).*

Muchelney Abbey

🏰 NUNNEY CASTLE 🏰

A small 14th century moated castle with a distinctly French style. Its unusual design consists of a central block with large round towers at the angles.

🕐 *Any reasonable time.*

♿ *(exterior only)* ⊗

➡ *In Nunney 3½m SW of Frome, off A361 (OS Map 183; ref ST 737457). Station: Frome 3½m.*

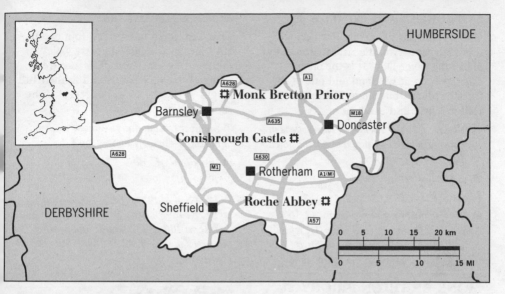

S OUTH YORKSHIRE is a metropolitan county, created out of the old West Riding. A centre of traditional industries, Sheffield has long been the home of cutlery manufacture, and parts of Yorkshire have been a traditional centre of coal mining. It is still a busy and developing county.

Yet in the centre of this modernity still sits a remarkable piece of medieval Yorkshire: Conisbrough Castle. Its mighty keep once stood in a forest that covered virtually the entire county. Near to Barnsley is the 12th century Monk Bretton Priory, and south lies Roche Abbey, its walls still standing to their full height.

Conisbrough Castle

CONISBROUGH CASTLE 🏰

The spectacular white circular keep of this 12th century castle rises majestically above the River Don. It is the oldest circular keep in England and one of the finest medieval buildings. There is a visitor centre and exhibition.

🕐 *All year. £1.50/£1.10/75p. (The castle is in the care of English Heritage and administered by the Ivanhoe Trust.)*

🅿 ⓑ *(limited access)* ⊗

✆ *(0709) 863329*

➥ *NE of Conisbrough town centre off A630, 4½m SW of Doncaster (OS Map 111; ref SK 515989). Bus: From surrounding areas (Tel: 0742 768688). Station: Conisbrough ½m.*

MONK BRETTON PRIORY 🏛

Partial sweeps of broken arches and grime-stained blocks of red sandstone mark the peaceful ruin of this Cluniac monastery founded in 1153.

🕐 *All year. 75p/55p/40p.*

🚻 *(Summer season)* 🅿 ⓑ 🗄 ⊗

✆ *(0226) 204089*

➥ *1m E of Barnsley town centre off A633 (OS Map 111; ref SE 373065). Bus: From surrounding areas (Tel: 0742 768688). Station: Barnsley 2½m.*

ROCHE ABBEY 🏛

This Cistercian monastery, founded in 1147, lies in a secluded grassy valley sheltered by limestone cliffs and trees. Some of the walls still stand to their full height and excavation has revealed the complete layout.

🕐 *Summer season, daily; Winter, weekends only, 10am-4pm. £1.10/85p/55p.*

🚻 🅿 🕯 ⓑ 🗄 ⊗

✆ *(0709) 812739*

➥ *1½m S of Maltby off A634 (OS Map 111; ref SK 544898). Bus: South Yorkshire Transport 100-2, 122 Rotherham-Maltby, thence 1½m (Tel: 0742 768688). Station: Conisbrough 7m.*

Roche Abbey

Monk Bretton Priory

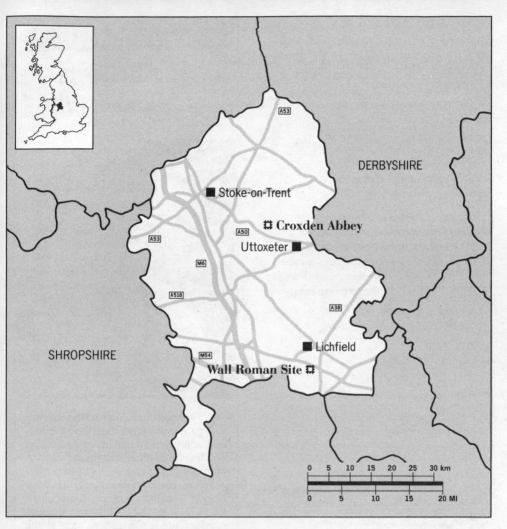

W HILE STAFFORDSHIRE'S REPUTATION is based on the Potteries and the Black Country, this tends to obscure the fact that Staffordshire's main industry is actually agriculture.

As well as a fascinating industrial heritage, the county is also rich in early history. At Wall, near Lichfield, are well-preserved Roman ruins which include a Roman roadside settlement where the remains of a bath and lodging house can be seen.

A few miles north of Uttoxeter lies Croxden Abbey. Set in a valley, Croxden was founded as a Cistercian abbey in the 12th century. Parts of the cloisters, west front and south transept still remain.

CROXDEN ABBEY

Remains of a Cistercian abbey founded in 1176. The east range of the cloisters survives, as do the west front and south transept of the church.

⏱ *Any reasonable time.*

⊛

➥ *5m NW of Uttoxeter off A50 (OS Map 128; ref SK 065397).* Station: *Uttoxeter 6m.*

WALL ROMAN SITE (LETOCETUM)

The remarkable achievements of the Romans are demonstrated by these remains of a staging post, alongside Watling Street. Foundations of an inn and bath house can be seen, and there is a display of finds in the site museum.

⏱ *All year. £1.10/85p/55p. (NT)*

🔊 ⊗ ♿

☎ *(0543) 480768*

➥ *Off A5 at Wall near Lichfield (OS Map 139; ref SK 099067).* Station: *Shenstone 1½m.*

Wall Roman Site

English ⌗ Heritage

The Benefits of Membership

As a member of English Heritage you gain much more than the benefit of free admission to our historic sites and buildings. You also enjoy the satisfaction of helping to preserve England's most important buildings for future generations. English Heritage protects conservation areas, lists buildings of historic value and provides funds for others, such as the National Trust, who are working to conserve the best of the past.

English Heritage Magazine, your quarterly member's journal, will keep adults and children in touch with the work we do as well as advise you of the many activities, events and opportunities available to members.

Being a member of English Heritage means much more than simply a free pass to some of England's most interesting places.

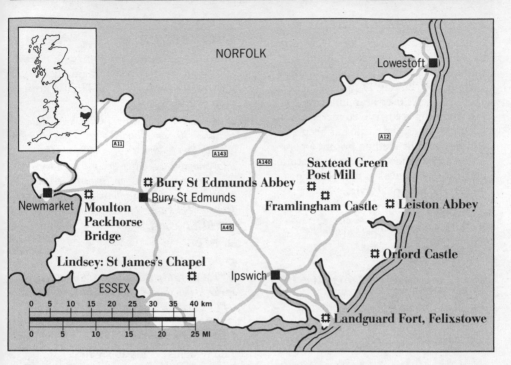

NORFOLK

Lowestoft

A11

A143

A140

A12

Saxtead Green
Post Mill

⌗ Bury St Edmunds Abbey

⌗ Bury St Edmunds

Newmarket

Moulton
Packhorse
Bridge

⌗ Framlingham Castle   ⌗ Leiston Abbey

A45

⌗ Orford Castle

Lindsey: St James's Chapel

Ipswich

ESSEX

| 0 | 5 | 10 | 15 | 20 | 25 | 30 | 35 | 40 km |

| 0 | 5 | 10 | 15 | 20 | 25 MI |

⌗ Landguard Fort, Felixstowe

SUFFOLK IS STILL A COUNTY left comparatively untouched by modern development. Many visitors will be familiar with the pink-walled thatched cottages which the area possesses in abundance. A county of small market centres, attractive villages and working fishing towns, Suffolk's gentle countryside provided a home for both Thomas Gainsborough and John Constable — and an inspiration for many of Constable's most famous paintings. Many of the landscapes chosen by Constable can still be seen, just as the painter saw them.

Yet despite its timeless quality, the tranquility of Suffolk is belied by the historic forces which shaped its contemporary form. From a background of occupation by both the Romans and Anglo-Saxons, the county's wealth grew spectacularly during the Middle Ages, providing the resources for the rich architectural bequest — both sacred and secular — on view to any visitor today.

BURY ST EDMUNDS ABBEY 🏚

The splendid 14th century gatehouse is the most evocative feature of this huge ruined Benedictine abbey. Substantial parts of the church remain, within the attractive town park.

🕐 Park opening hours (borough council).

♿

➡ E end of town centre (OS Map 155; ref TL 858642). Bus: From surrounding areas (Tel: 0473 265676). Station: Bury St Edmunds 1m.

FRAMLINGHAM CASTLE ☒

A superb 12th century castle which, from the outside, looks almost the same as when it was built. From the continuous curtain wall, linking 13 towers, there are excellent views over Framlingham and the charming reed-fringed mere. At different times, the castle has been a fortress, an Elizabethan prison, a poor house and a school. The many alterations over the years have led to a pleasing mixture of historical styles.

🕐 *All year. £1.50/£1.10/75p.*

⊗ 🖹 🗋 🅿 ♿ *(grounds & ground floor only)* 🗋 ⓜ

✆ *(0728) 724189*

➡ *In Framlingham on B1116 (OS Map 156; ref TM 287637). Bus: Eastern Counties 80/2/ 3 from Ipswich (pass close BR Wickham Market) (Tel: 0473 265676). Station: Wickham Market 6½m.*

Framlingham Castle

LANDGUARD FORT, FELIXSTOWE ☒

Impressive 18th century fort, with later additions, built on a site originally fortified by Henry VIII and in use until after World War II.

🕐 *Museum open 31 May-4 Oct, Wed, Thur & Sun 2.30-5pm. Guided tours of fort museum Wed & Sun 2.45pm & 4pm. 80p/50p (no unaccompanied children or concessionary rates. We regret no reduction for English Heritage members.) For further information tel. Mrs D Rayner (Felixstowe Historical Society): (0394) 286403 (evenings).*

🅿 ⊗ ⓜ

➡ *1m S of Felixstowe near docks (OS Map 169; ref TM 284318). Bus: Eastern Counties 75-9 Ipswich-Felixstowe Dock to within ¾m. (Tel: 0473 253734). Station: Felixstowe 2½m.*

LEISTON ABBEY ☒

The remains of this abbey for Premonstratensian canons, including a restored chapel, are among the most extensive in Suffolk.

🕐 *Any reasonable time.*

🅿 ♿ ⊗

➡ *1m N of Leiston off B1069 (OS Map 156; ref TM 445642). Bus: Eastern Counties 80-2, X80, 142/3 Ipswich-Aldeburgh (pass close BR Saxmundham) (Tel: 0473 265676). Station: Saxmundham 5m.*

LINDSEY: ST JAMES'S CHAPEL 🏛

A little 13th century chapel with thatched roof and lancet windows.

🕐 *All year.*

⊗ ♿ *(single step).*

➲ *On unclassified road ½m E of Rose Green, 8m E of Sudbury (OS Map 155; ref TL 978443).* Bus: *Norfolk 139, Suffolk Sunday Bus 144/5 from Ipswich, Sat, Sun only (Tel: 0473 265676).* Station: *Sudbury 8m.*

MOULTON PACKHORSE BRIDGE

Medieval four-arched bridge spanning the River Kennet on the ancient route from Bury St Edmunds to Cambridge.

🕐 *Any reasonable time.*

🅿 ♿ ⊗

➲ *In Moulton off B1085, 4m E of Newmarket (OS Map 154; ref TL 698645).* Station: *Kennet 2m.*

ORFORD CASTLE 🏰

A royal castle built for coastal defence in the 12th century. A magnificent keep survives almost intact with three immense towers reaching to 90 feet. Inside there are many rooms to explore.

🕐 *All year. £1.50/£1.10/75p.*

🅿 ⊗ ▯

☎ *(03944) 50472*

➲ *In Orford on B1084 20m NE of Ipswich (OS Map 169; ref TM 419499).* Bus: *Belle 1, Eastern Counties 122 Woodbridge-Orford (passes close BR Woodbridge) (Tel: 0473 265676).* Station: *Wickham Market 8m.*

SAXTEAD GREEN POST MILL 🌾

The finest example of a Suffolk post mill. Still in working order, you can climb the wooden stairs to the various floors, full of fascinating mill machinery.

🕐 *Summer season, Mon-Sat 10am-6pm. £1.10/85p/55p.*

⊗

☎ *(0728) 685789*

➲ *2½m NW of Framlingham on A1120 (OS Map 156; ref TM 253645).* Station: *Wickham Market 9m.*

Saxtead Green Post Mill

Orford Castle

SURREY

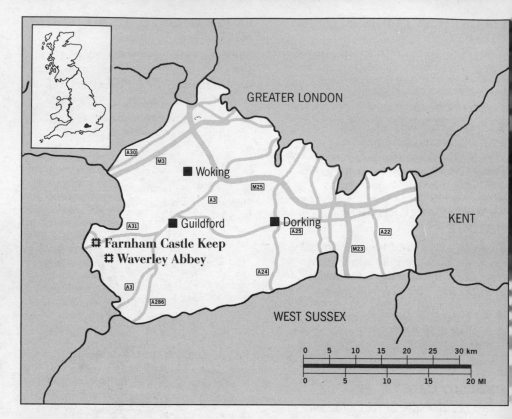

IT IS EASY TO FORGET that Surrey begins close to the heart of London. Almost immediately it adopts a rural character. The expanses of Richmond Park and Bushy Park, and the genteel stretch of the Thames from Kew to Twickenham have a calm country air which belie their proximity to the centre of the city.

Further out from London, Surrey's rural charm is unequivocal. The North Downs provide some beautiful scenery, including the Hog's Back near Guildford, which affords panoramic views of the county and beyond.

Surrey also has some very picturesque towns, including Farnham, with its elegant Georgian houses. Just outside of the town is Farnham Castle Keep, a former residence of the Bishops of Winchester. Nearby is another historic religious foundation, Waverley Abbey — the earliest Cistercian house in England.

136

⚜ FARNHAM CASTLE KEEP 🏰

Used as a fortified manor by the medieval Bishops of Winchester, this motte and bailey castle has been in continuous occupation since the 12th century. You can visit the large shell-keep enclosing a mound in which are massive foundations of a Norman tower.

☼ *Summer season. £1.40/£1/70p.*

🅿 🎧 ♿

✆ *(0252) 713393*

➡ *½m N of Farnham town centre on A287 (OS Map 186; ref SU 839474).* Bus: *From surrounding areas (Tel: 0483 575226).* Station: *Farnham ¾m.*

Farnham Castle Keep

WAVERLEY ABBEY 🏚

This was the first Cistercian house in England, founded in 1128. The remaining ruins date from the 13th century and can be found in a beautiful setting by the River Wey.

☼ *Any reasonable time.*

🅿 *(limited)* ♿

➡ *2m SE of Farnham off B3001 (OS Map 186; ref SU 868453).* Station: *Farnham 2m.*

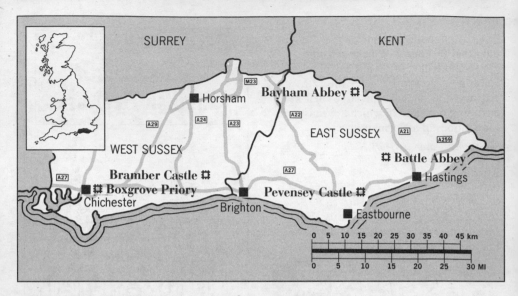

IN 1066 WILLIAM THE CONQUEROR landed in Sussex at Pevensey. He then marched to a site near Hastings and defeated King Harold, irrevocably changing the course of English history.

Following his victory, William built an abbey near the site of the battle. Its impressive gatehouse still stands. The battlefield nearby can also be visited. At Pevensey there are the ruins of a medieval castle, enclosed within an earlier Roman fort.

Beyond Hastings lie the resort towns of Brighton and Eastbourne. Behind them are the Sussex Downs, with rolling open green countryside, as undeveloped as any upland district in England.

Battle Abbey

BATTLE ABBEY AND SITE OF THE BATTLE OF HASTINGS 🏛

You can explore the actual battlefield, stand where Harold's men stood and see where William the Conqueror's horsemen turned the tide of battle and won the day. The abbey was founded c.1070 by William to atone for the bloodshed with the high altar built on the very spot where King Harold fell. There are well preserved remains of the cloister buildings of the abbey, and the magnificent 14th century Gatehouse is now open to the public, housing a new museum which traces the history of the site from the Battle of Hastings through to the conversion of the abbey to a country house in the 16th century.

⏲ *All year, plus Mondays in Winter. Visitor centre with audiovisual — '1066, The Battle of Hastings'; Abbot's Hall open to public school summer holidays only. £2.50/£1.90/£1.30.*

🅿 *(charge payable)* 🎧 ⅄ *(some steps)* 🚻 🛇 🚻 🚻 🎵

✆ *(04246) 3792*

➡ *At S end of Battle High St (OS Map 199; ref TQ 749157). Bus: Hastings Buses/Maidstone & District 4/5 Maidstone-Hastings (Tel: 0634 832666). Station: Battle ½m.*

BRAMBER CASTLE 🏰

The remains of a Norman castle gatehouse, walls and earthworks in a splendid setting overlooking the Adur valley.

⏲ *Any reasonable time. (NT)*

🅿 *(limited)* 🛇

➡ *On W side of Bramber village off A283 (OS Map 198; ref TQ 187107). Bus: Brighton & Hove 20 BR Shoreham-by-Sea — Steyning (Tel: 0273 206666). Station: Shoreham-by-Sea 4½m.*

BOXGROVE PRIORY 🏛

Remains of the Guest House, Chapter House and church of this 12th century priory, which was the cell of a French abbey until Richard II confirmed its independence in 1383.

⏲ *Any reasonable time.*

🛇 🅿

➡ *N of Boxgrove, 4m E of Chichester on minor road off A27. (OS Map 197; ref SU 909076). Bus: Southdown 268/9 from BR Chichester (Tel: 0243 783251). Station: Chichester 4m.*

BAYHAM ABBEY 🏛

These riverside ruins are of a house of 'white' canons, founded c.1208 and preserved in the 18th century, when its surroundings were landscaped to create the delightful setting in which you will find the ruins today.

⏲ *Summer season. £1.50/£1.10/75p.*

🚻 🅿 ⅄ 🛇

✆ *(0892) 890381*

➡ *1¾m W of Lamberhurst off B2169 (OS Map 188; ref TQ 651366). Bus: Warrens 256 BR Tunbridge Wells-Wadhurst (Tel: 0580 200226). Station: Frant 4m.*

Bayham Abbey

PEVENSEY CASTLE ⛫

This medieval castle includes the remains of an unusual keep enclosed within its walls which originally date back to the 4th century Roman fort Anderida.

🕐 *All year. £1.50/£1.10/75p.*

🅿 *(charge payable)* ♿ ♀♂ *(nearby)* 🍴 ⊗ ♿

✆ *(0323) 762604*

➡ *In Pevensey (OS Map 199; ref TQ 645048). Bus: Eastbourne Buses 28, Hastings Buses 99 from Eastbourne (Tel: 0273 478007). Station: Pevensey & Westham or Pevensey Bay, both ½m.*

Pevensey Castle

Scene from new interactive video at Battle.

English ⌗ Heritage

New exhibition at Battle Abbey

Battle Abbey, founded by William the Conqueror soon after the Battle of Hastings, has a unique place in England's history.

Now its story has been told in a major new exhibition in the Abbey's Gatehouse, that takes you on a journey through more than 900 years of history.

You can find out what problems the monks encountered in building William's abbey after 1066, discover the secrets and skills of the medieval craftsmen who built it, take a close look at the daily life of a monastery and much more besides.

And now that we've opened the acres of parkland beside the abbey to visitors, you can even take a picnic and make your visit to Battle Abbey a real family day out.

See page 139 for opening times and directions.

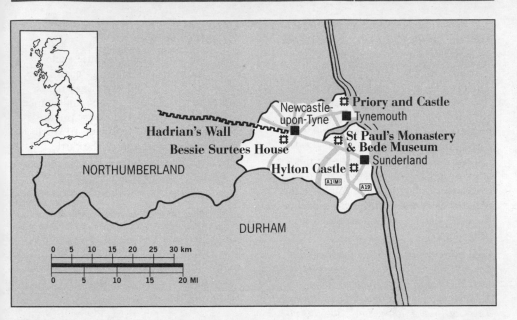

TYNE AND WEAR, a tiny county, has several monuments and attractions worth seeking out. The eastern end of Hadrian's Wall finishes near Newcastle upon Tyne, and small parts can still be seen in the city's suburbs.

In Jarrow, the 8th century monastery which was home to the Venerable Bede survives as part of the local parish church. The castles at Hylton and Tynemouth are also well worth a visit.

BESSIE SURTEES HOUSE ⌂

Two 16th and 17th century merchants' houses stand on the quayside near the Tyne Bridge. One is a remarkable and rare example of Jacobean domestic architecture. The principal rooms are on view and you will also find the English Heritage Regional Information Centre here.

⊙ *All year, plus Mondays in Winter.*

⍮ ⊗

✆ *091-261 1585*

➲ *41-44 Sandhill, Newcastle. (OS Map 88; ref NZ 252639). Bus: From surrounding areas (Tel: 091-232 5325). Station: Newcastle ½m. Metro: Central Station ½m.*

HYLTON CASTLE ⍟

This is a 15th century keep-gatehouse, set in wooded parkland, with a fine display of medieval heraldry adorning the facades. The 15th-16th century St Catherine's Chapel stands nearby.

⊙ *All year. 75p/55p/40p.*

🅿 ♿ *(grounds only)* ⊗

✆ *091-548 0752*

➲ *3¾m W of Sunderland (OS Map 88; ref NZ 358588). Bus: From surrounding areas (Tel: 091-232 5325). Station: Seaburn 2½m.*

ST PAUL'S MONASTERY AND BEDE MONASTERY MUSEUM, JARROW 🏛

The home of the Venerable Bede in the 7th and 8th centuries, partly surviving as the chancel of the parish church. Recently excavated, the monastery has become one of the best-understood Anglo-Saxon monastic sites.

Built c.1800, the Museum tells the story of St Paul's Monastery, and displays excavated finds, including Anglo-Saxon window glass and sculpture, a model of the early monastery and an audio-visual programme.

⏱ Monastery ruins open at any reasonable time, free admission. Museum open 1 April-31 Oct: Tues-Sat & Bank Holidays 10am-5.50pm, Sun 2.30-5.30pm; 1 Nov-31 March: Tues-Sat 11am-4.30pm, Sun 2.30-5.30pm. Closed Christmas — New Year. Adults 60p/ Senior Citizens, Children 30p/Students 40p/ UB40 30p (75p with family).

🍴 ⅋ 🚻 ⅋. 🗁 🛍 ☯ *(Monastery only; no dogs allowed to Museum)* 🅜

☎ 091-489 2106

➲ In Jarrow, on minor road N of A185 (OS Map 88; ref NZ 339652). Bus: *Go-Ahead Northern 527 Newcastle-upon-Tyne — South Shields.* Metro: *Bede ¾m.*

🏰 TYNEMOUTH CASTLE AND PRIORY 🏰 🏛

The castle walls and gatehouse enclose the substantial remains of a Benedictine priory founded c.1090 on a Saxon monastic site. Their strategic importance has made the castle and priory the target for attack for many centuries. In World War I, coastal batteries in the castle defended the mouth of the Tyne.

⏱ All year; gun battery open from noon Fri-Mon. £1.10/85p/55p.

🗁 🚻 *(local council)* ⅋. *(castle)* 🛍 ☯

☎ 091-257 1090

➲ In Tynemouth, near North Pier (OS Map 88; ref NZ 374695). Bus: *From surrounding areas (Tel: 091-232 5325).* Metro: *Tynemouth ½m.*

Tynemouth Priory

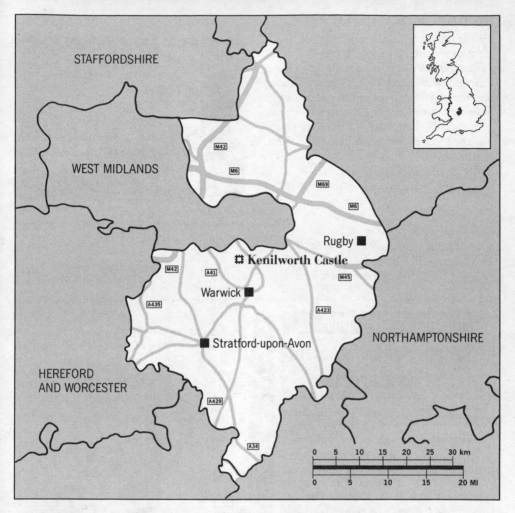

STAFFORDSHIRE

WEST MIDLANDS

M42
M6
M69
M6

Rugby ■

⌗ **Kenilworth Castle**

M42
A41
A45

Warwick ■

A435
A423

NORTHAMPTONSHIRE

■ Stratford-upon-Avon

HEREFORD
AND WORCESTER

A429

A34

```
0   5   10  15  20  25  30 km
0   5      10      15   20 MI
```

WARWICKSHIRE HAS a soft undulating rural landscape, characterised by elegant towns and small fields bounded by hedgerows and streams. With the creation of the metropolitan county of the West Midlands in 1974, Warwickshire's rural character has become even more pronounced.

Rich in places of historical interest, Warwickshire includes Shakespeare's Stratford-upon-Avon, and the beautiful town of Warwick, with its impressive castle.

Another medieval castle is nearby, at Kenilworth, one of the most extensive in Britain. Begun in the 12th century it was extended right up until the 17th century, with major additions in the reign of Elizabeth I. Built of rich, warm, red sandstone, it inspired Sir Walter Scott's famous novel, *Kenilworth*.

KENILWORTH CASTLE

The dramatic red sandstone ruins of this great castle rise above rich green pastureland, with massive walls up to 20 feet thick and a 12th century keep. There are impressive remains of the state rooms built and furnished for Elizabeth I's visits by Robert Dudley, Earl of Leicester, who was the Queen's favourite. There is a site exhibition.

All year. £1.50/£1.10/75p.

(0926) 52078

➡ *In Kenilworth (OS Map 140; ref SP 278723). Bus: Midland Red X16/7/9, 18; G & G X12, 63 BR Coventry-Leamington Spa (Tel: 0788 535555). Station: Warwick 5m.*

Kenilworth Castle

English ♯ Heritage

Summer entertainment at Kenilworth

Kenilworth provides an imposing setting for a rich variety of events taking place throughout the summer.

There's opera in the open air from Opera Box, a talented company of professional singers from Britain's finest opera houses. This year on 1 August they are performing Weber's *Der Freischütz* while the following evening brings the ever popular *Magic Flute* by Mozart to the stage.

There's another chance, too, to enjoy our popular Henry VIII display which includes an uncannily believable portrayal of the great King himself. We shall also be presenting a series of medieval entertainments and some fascinating falconry displays.

Phone (0926) 52078 for more details and booking information.

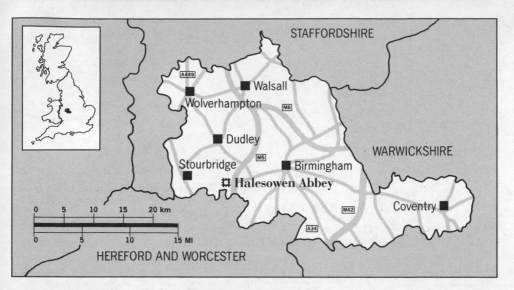

STAFFORDSHIRE

A449

■ Walsall

Wolverhampton

M6

■ Dudley

WARWICKSHIRE

M5

Stourbridge ■

■ Birmingham

✠ **Halesowen Abbey**

M42

Coventry ■

A34

| 0 | 5 | 10 | 15 | 20 km |

| 0 | 5 | 10 | 15 MI |

HEREFORD AND WORCESTER

THE WEST MIDLANDS was formed from parts of Warwickshire, Staffordshire and Worcestershire as part of the reorganisation of local government in 1974. Aspects of each of these counties still survive, though an identity of its own is beginning to emerge.

Densely populated, the county is dominated by the two industrial cities of Coventry and Birmingham. Coventry suffered severely from bombing during World War II, yet many buildings of historic importance remain.

Six miles to the west of Birmingham sit the remains of Halesowen Abbey, founded in the 13th century.

HALESOWEN ABBEY 🏛

Remains of an abbey founded by King John in the 13th century, now incorporated into a 19th century farm. Parts of the church and monks' infirmary can still be made out.

⏱ *2 June-31 Aug, Sundays & Bank Holidays only 10am-6pm. 60p/45p/35p.*

🅿 ⊗ ♿ *(rough grass between church and infirmary).*

➡ *Off A456 Kidderminster road, 6m W of Birmingham city centre. (OS Map 139; ref SO 975828). Bus: West Midlands Travel 9, 19 Birmingham-Stourbridge (Tel: 021-200 2700). Station: Old Hill 2½m.*

Halesowen Abbey

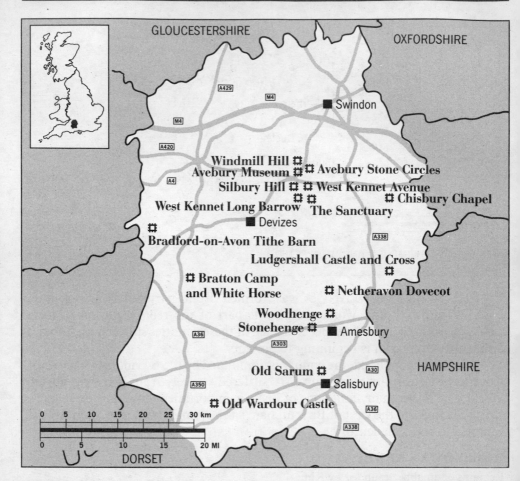

GLOUCESTERSHIRE

OXFORDSHIRE

Swindon

Windmill Hill
Avebury Museum ⌗ ⌗ Avebury Stone Circles
Silbury Hill ⌗ ⌗ West Kennet Avenue
West Kennet Long Barrow ⌗ ⌗ ⌗ Chisbury Chapel
The Sanctuary
Devizes
⌗ Bradford-on-Avon Tithe Barn
Ludgershall Castle and Cross
⌗ Bratton Camp ⌗
and White Horse ⌗ Netheravon Dovecot
Woodhenge ⌗
Stonehenge ⌗ Amesbury
Old Sarum ⌗
Salisbury
⌗ Old Wardour Castle

HAMPSHIRE

0 5 10 15 20 25 30 km
0 5 10 15 20 MI

DORSET

WILTSHIRE'S LANDSCAPE is dotted with prehistoric monuments. Rising dramatically from the centre of Salisbury Plain is the world famous stone circle at Stonehenge, standing sentinel for around five thousand years.

In the north of the county lies Avebury. The stone circles here are part of a larger prehistoric complex, which includes The Sanctuary, West Kennet Long Barrow, Silbury and Windmill Hills, and an ancient avenue. The meaning of many of these monuments remains obscure, but Avebury Museum nearby may help shed some light.

The slender spire of the magnificent 13th century cathedral in Salisbury is the highest in England. The remains of its predecessor can be seen among the ruins at Old Sarum. There is also an excellent tithe barn from the same period at the historic town of Bradford-on-Avon.

AVEBURY STONE CIRCLES ⋔

Complex, gigantic and mysterious, originally comprising more than 180 stones, the remains of the Circles, constructed 4,000 years ago, still surround the later village of Avebury.

⊕ *Any reasonable time. (NT)*

⋔ *(in village)* **P** ♿ ⊗ ⊡ *(in car park)*

➡ *In Avebury 7m W of Marlborough (OS Map 173; ref SU 103700). Bus: Thamesdown 49 Swindon-Devizes/Marlborough; Wilts & Dorset 5 Salisbury-Swindon (Tel: 0345 090 899). Both pass close BR Swindon. Station: Pewsey 10m, Swindon 11m.*

Avebury Stone Circles

AVEBURY MUSEUM

The investigation of Avebury Stone Circles was largely the work of Alexander Keiller in the 1930's. He put together one of the most important prehistoric archaeological collections in Britain, and this can be seen in the Avebury Museum.

⊕ *All year, plus Mondays in Winter. £1.20/ 90p/60p.*

⋔ **P** ⊗ ♿ ▤ ⊡

☎ *(06723) 250*

➡ *In Avebury 7m W of Marlborough (OS Map 173; ref SU 100700). Bus: Thamesdown 49 Swindon-Devizes/Marlborough; Wilts & Dorset 5 Salisbury-Swindon (Tel: 0345 090 899). Both pass close BR Swindon. Station: Pewsey 10m, Swindon 11m.*

AVEBURY ⋔

See also *The Sanctuary, Silbury Hill, West Kennet Avenue, West Kennet Long Barrow* and *Windmill Hill.*

BRADFORD-ON-AVON TITHE BARN

A magnificent medieval stone-built barn with slate roof and wooden beamed interior.

⊕ *Any reasonable time. Keykeeper.*

P ♿ ⊗

☎ *Area Office (0272) 734472*

➡ *¼m S of town centre, off B3109. (OS Map 173; ref ST 824604). Bus: Badgerline X4 Bristol-Salisbury, 264/5 Bath-Frome (Tel: 0225 464446). Station: Bradford-on-Avon ¼m.*

Bradford-on-Avon Tithe Barn

BRATTON CAMP AND WHITE HORSE 🏛

There are wonderful views from this large Iron Age hill fort, particularly of the splendid White Horse which was cut in its present form in 1778.

⊕ *Any reasonable time.*

P ⊛

➲ *2m E of Westbury off B3098, 1m SW of Bratton. (OS Map 184; ref ST 900516). Station: Westbury 3m.*

CHISBURY CHAPEL ⛪

A thatched 13th century chapel recently rescued from use as a farm building.

⊕ *Any reasonable time.*

⊛

➲ *On unclassified road off A4 6m E of Marlborough. (OS Map 174; ref SU 280658). Station: Bedwyn 1m.*

LUDGERSHALL CASTLE AND CROSS 🏰

Ruins of an early 12th century royal hunting palace with an obscure history. The late medieval cross stands in the main street of the village.

⊕ *Any reasonable time.*

P *(limited)* ♿ *(part of site only & village cross)* ⊛

➲ *On N side of Ludgershall off A342. (OS Map 184; ref SU 264513). Bus: Hampshire Bus/Wilts & Dorset 7-9 BR Andover-Salisbury (Tel: 0264 352339). Station: Andover 7m.*

NETHERAVON DOVECOTE

A charming 18th century brick dovecote, standing in a pleasant orchard, with most of its 700 or more nesting boxes still present.

⊕ *Exterior viewing only, by written application to English Heritage (South West Region), Keysign House, 429 Oxford Street, London W1R 2HD.*

⊛

➲ *In Netheravon, 4½m N of Amesbury on A345. (OS Map 184; ref SU 146485). Bus: Wilts & Dorset 5/6 Salisbury-Swindon (pass close BR Salisbury & Swindon). (Tel: 0722 336855). Station: Pewsey 9m, Grateley 11m.*

OLD SARUM 🏰

First an Iron Age fort, later inhabited by Romans, Saxons, Danes and Normans, there is much to disentangle from the 56 acres of ruins at this fascinating site. The Normans created a castle, the first Salisbury Cathedral and the Bishop's Palace. From the castle ramparts there are fine views of the surrounding countryside.

⊕ *All year. £1.20/90p/60p.*

🚻 **P** ♿ *(inner bailey & grounds only)* ⊛

✆ *(0722) 335398*

➲ *2m N of Salisbury off A345 (OS Map 184; ref SU 138327). Bus: Wilts & Dorset/ Hampshire Bus 3, 5-9, X19 from Salisbury (Tel: 0722 336855). Station: Salisbury 2m.*

Old Sarum

OLD WARDOUR CASTLE

In a picture-book setting, the unusual hexagonal ruins of this 14th century castle stand on the edge of a beautiful lake, surrounded by landscaped grounds which include an elaborate rockwork grotto.

Summer season, daily; Winter, weekends only, 10am-4pm. £1.20/90p/60p.

(grounds only)

(0747) 870487

Off A30 2m SW of Tisbury. (OS Map 184; ref ST 939263). Station: Tisbury 2½m.

Old Wardour Castle

STONEHENGE

One piece of magic that never fails to cast a spell over the traveller is the awe-inspiring site of this famous prehistoric monument as one crosses Salisbury Plain. Started 5,000 years ago, we can only really apply supposition and guess-work to interpret the reasons for its existence, but we do know that the prehistoric builders went to incredible lengths to construct such a monument. The massive stone lintels are mortice-and-tenoned to the uprights upon which they rest, and are curved to follow a circle. Some of the stones weigh over 50 tons each, with some brought from the Preseli Mountains in Wales. Even if we remain unclear about its purpose, we can admire this extraordinary achievement of the earliest inhabitants of these islands.

All year, plus Mondays in Winter. £2.50/ £1.90/£1.30. (NT)

Area office (0272) 734472

2m W of Amesbury on junction A303 and A344/A360. (OS Map 184; ref SU 123422). Bus: Wilts & Dorset 3 BR Salisbury-Stonehenge (Tel: 0722 336855). Station: Salisbury 9½m.

Stonehenge

THE SANCTUARY ⋔

A prehistoric monument, possibly 5,000 years old, consisting of two concentric circles of stones and six of timber uprights indicated by concrete posts, connected to Avebury by the West Kennet Avenue of standing stones.

🕐 *Any reasonable time.*

🕭

➥ *Beside A4, ½m E of West Kennet. (OS Map 173, ref SU 118679).* Bus: *Thamesdown 49 Swindon-Marlborough; Wilts & Dorset 5 Salisbury-Swindon (Tel: 0345 090 899. Both pass close BR Swindon.* Station: *Pewsey 9m, Bedwyn 12m.*

SILBURY HILL ⋔

An extraordinary artificial prehistoric mound, with no obvious purpose but nevertheless the largest Neolithic construction of its type in Europe.

🕐 *Any reasonable time (no access to the hill itself).*

� *(viewing area)* 🕭

➥ *1m W of West Kennet on A4. (OS Map 173; ref SU 100685).* Bus: *Thamesdown 49 Swindon-Devizes/Marlborough; Wilts & Dorset 5 Salisbury-Swindon (Tel: 0345 090 899). Both pass close BR Swindon.* Station: *Pewsey 9m, Swindon 13m.*

WEST KENNET AVENUE, AVEBURY ⋔

An avenue of standing stones which ran in a curve from Avebury Stone Circles to The Sanctuary, probably dating from the late Neolithic Age.

🕐 *Any reasonable time. (NT)*

⅛ *(on roadway)* 🕭

➥ *Runs alongside B4003. (OS Map 173; ref SU 105695).* Bus: *Thamesdown 49 Swindon-Marlborough; Wilts & Dorset 5 Salisbury-Swindon (Tel: 0345 090 899).* Both pass close *BR Swindon.* Station: *Pewsey 9m, Swindon 12m.*

WEST KENNET LONG BARROW ⋔

One of the largest Neolithic chambered tombs of its type, consisting of a long earthen mound containing a passage with side chambers, and with the entrance guarded by a large stone.

🕐 *Any reasonable time.*

🅿 *(in layby)* 🕭

➥ *¾m SW of West Kennet along footpath off A4. (OS Map 173; ref SU 104677).* Bus: *Thamesdown 49 Swindon-Marlborough; Wilts & Dorset 5 Salisbury-Swindon (Tel: 0345 090 899). Both to within 1m. Both pass close BR Swindon.* Station: *Pewsey 9m, Swindon 13m.*

WINDMILL HILL

The Neolithic remains of three concentric rings of ditches which enclosed an area of 21 acres and which may have been a market or tribal centre.

🕐 *Any reasonable time. (NT)*

🚻

➥ *1½m NW of Avebury. (OS Map 173; ref SU 086714).* Bus: *Thamesdown 49 Swindon-Devizes/Marlborough; Wilts & Dorset 5 Salisbury-Swindon (Tel: 0345 090 899). Both to within 1m. Both pass close BR Swindon.* Station: *Swindon 11m.*

WOODHENGE

Neolithic ceremonial monument of c.2300BC, consisting of six concentric rings of timber posts, now marked by concrete piles. The long axis of the rings, which are oval, points to the rising sun on Midsummer Day.

🕐 *Any reasonable time.*

🅿 ♿ 🚻

➥ *1½m N of Amesbury, off A345 just S of Durrington. (OS Map 184; ref SU 151434).* Bus: *Wilts & Dorset 5/6 Salisbury-Swindon (pass close BR Salisbury & Swindon). (Tel: 0722 336855).* Station: *Salisbury 9m.*

English ♯ Heritage

Summer spectacle in Hardy Country

"Hardy's Wessex at Old Sarum", taking place on June 27 and 28, will take you back to 1870, when Thomas Hardy had begun writing his novels of the Wessex countryside.

You can spend the day in the company of Victorian countryfolk and there'll be music, dancing and entertainments of every description.

Bring a picnic, come along in period costume if you wish, and make the most of this charming re-creation of Victorian England.

You'll find full details in your 1992 Events Diary and don't forget that admission is free if you're a member of English Heritage.

INDEX

Abbotsbury Abbey Remains 43
Abbotsbury: St Catherine's Chapel 45
Abingdon County Hall 119
Acton Burnell Castle 122
Agricola Tower and Castle Walls,
    Chester 22
Aldborough Roman Town 111
Ambleside Roman Fort 30
Appuldurcombe House 80
Arbor Low Stone Circle & Gib Hill
    Barrow 36
Arthur's Round Table 30
Arthur's Stone, Dorstone 74
Ashby de la Zouch Castle 95
Auckland Castle Deer House, Bishop
    Auckland 46
Audley End House and Park 48
Avebury Museum 147
Avebury Stone Circles 147
Avebury: The Sanctuary 150
Aydon Castle 106

Baconsthorpe Castle 98
Ballowall Barrow, St Just 25
Banks East Turret 61
Bant's Carn Burial Chamber and Halangy
    Down Ancient Village 83
Barnard Castle 47
Barrow-in-Furness: Bow Bridge 30
Barton-upon-Humber: St Peter's
    Church 78
Battle Abbey and site of the Battle of
    Hastings 139
Bayard's Cove Fort 40
Bayham Abbey 139
Beeston Castle 21
Belas Knap Long Barrow 51
Belsay Hall, Castle and Gardens 106
Benwell Roman Temple 61
Benwell Vallum Crossing 61
Berkhamsted Castle 76
Berney Arms Windmill 99
Berry Pomeroy Castle 39
Berwick-upon-Tweed Barracks 106
Berwick-upon-Tweed Castle 107
Berwick-upon-Tweed Ramparts 107
Bessie Surtees House 141
Binham Priory 99
Binham Wayside Cross 99
Birdoswald Fort, Wall and Turret 61
Bishop Auckland: Auckland Castle Deer
    House 46

Bishop's Palace, Lincoln 96
Bishop's Waltham Palace 67
Blackbury Camp 39
Black Carts Turret 62
Blackfriars, Gloucester 52
Black Middens Bastle House 107
Blakeney Guildhall 99
Bolingbroke Castle 97
Bolsover Castle 36
Boscobel House and the Royal Oak 122
Bow Bridge, Barrow-in-Furness 30
Bowes Castle 46
Bowhill 39
Boxgrove Priory 139
Bradford-on-Avon Tithe Barn 147
Bramber Castle 139
Bratton Camp and White Horse 148
Brinkburn Priory 107
Bristol: Temple Church 14
Brougham Castle 30
Brougham: Countess Pillar 31
Brough Castle 30
Brunton Turret 62
Buildwas Abbey 122
Burgh Castle 99
Burton Agnes Manor House 78
Bury St Edmunds Abbey 133
Bushmead Priory 17
Butter Cross, Dunster 127
Byland Abbey 111

Caister Roman Site 99
Callington: Dupath Well 25
Calshot Castle 67
Canterbury: St Augustine's Abbey 90
Cantlop Bridge 122
Carisbrooke Castle 80
Carlisle Castle 31
Carn Euny Ancient Village 25
Carrawburgh: Temple of Mithras 62
Castle Acre Bailey Gate 100
Castle Acre Castle 100
Castle Acre Priory 100
Castlerigg Stone Circle 31
Castle Rising Castle 100
Cawfields Roman Wall and Milecastle 62
Chester Castle: Agricola Tower and Castle
    Walls 22
Chester Roman Amphitheatre 22
Chesters Bridge Abutment 62
Chesters Fort and Museum 62
Chichele College 103

Chisbury Chapel 148
Chiswick House 56
Christchurch Castle and Norman
  House 43
Church of the Holy Sepulchre,
  Thetford 102
Chysauster Ancient Village 25
Cirencester Amphitheatre 52
Cleeve Abbey 126
Clifford's Tower, York 111
Clifton Hall 32
Clun Castle 123
Colchester: Lexden Earthworks and
  Bluebottle Grove 49
Colchester: St Botolph's Priory 49
Colchester: St John's Abbey Gate 49
Conisbrough Castle 130
Corbridge Roman Site 63
Countess Pillar, Brougham 31
Cow Tower, Norwich 102
Creake Abbey 101
Cromwell's Castle 83
Croxden Abbey 132

Dartmoor: Grimspound 39
Dartmoor: Hound Tor Deserted Medieval
  Village 39
Dartmoor: Merrivale Prehistoric
  Settlement 40
Dartmouth: Bayard's Cove Fort 40
Dartmouth Castle 40
Deal Castle 85
Deddington Castle 119
Deerhurst: Odda's Chapel 53
De Grey Mausoleum 17
Denny Abbey 20
Denton Hall Turret and West Denton 63
Derwentcote Steel Furnace 47
Donnington Castle 18
Dorstone: Arthur's Stone 74
Dover Castle 85
Dover: Knights Templar Church 86
Dover: Western Heights 86
Dragon Hill 120
Dunstanburgh Castle 108
Dunster: Butter Cross 127
Dunster: Gallox Bridge 127
Dunster: Yarn Market 127
Dupath Well House, Callington 25
Duxford Chapel 20
Dymchurch Martello Tower no 24 86

Easby Abbey 112

Ebbsfleet: St Augustine's Cross 90
Edlingham Castle 108
Edvin Loach Old Church 74
Egglestone Abbey 47
Eleanor Cross, Geddington 104
Eltham Palace 56
Etal Castle 108
Eynsford Castle 87

Farleigh Hungerford Castle 127
Farnham Castle Keep 137
Faversham Stone Chapel 87
Felixstowe: Landguard Fort 134
Fiddleford Manor 44
Finchale Priory 47
Flowerdown Barrows 67
Fort Brockhurst 68
Fowey: St Catherine's Castle 27
Framlingham Castle 134
Furness Abbey 32

Gainsborough Old Hall 97
Gainsthorpe Deserted Medieval Village 78
Gallox Bridge, Dunster 127
Garrison Church, Portsmouth 70
Garrison Walls 83
Geddington: Eleanor Cross 104
Gilsland Vicarage Roman Wall 63
Gisborough Priory 23
Glastonbury Tribunal 128
Gloucester: Blackfriars 52
Gloucester: Greyfriars 52
Goodrich Castle 74
Goodshaw Chapel 93
Grange, The, Northington 68
Gravesend: Milton Chantry 88
Great Witcombe Roman Villa 52
Great Yarmouth: Greyfriars' Cloister 101
Great Yarmouth: Old Merchant's House
  and Row 111 Houses 101
Greyfriars' Cloister, Great Yarmouth 101
Greyfriars, Gloucester 52
Grime's Graves 101
Grimspound 39

Hadleigh Castle 49
Hadrian's Wall 60-65
Hailes Abbey 52
Halesowen Abbey 145
Halliggye Fogou 25
Hardknott Roman Fort 32
Hardwick Old Hall 36

INDEX

Hare Hill 63
Harrow's Scar Milecastle 63
Harry's Walls 83
Hastings, site of Battle of 139
Haughmond Abbey 123
Heddon-on-the-Wall 63
Hellfire Corner 86
Helmsley Castle 112
Hetty Pegler's Tump (Uley Long
  Barrow) 54
Hob Hurst's House 36
Horne's Place Chapel, Appledore 87
Houghton House 17
Hound Tor Deserted Medieval Village 39
Housesteads Roman Fort 64
Hurlers Stone Circle 26
Hurst Castle 68
Hylton Castle 141

Innisidgen Lower and Upper Burial
  Chambers 83
Iron Bridge 123
Isleham Priory Church 20

Jarrow: St Paul's Monastery and Bede
  Museum 142
Jewel Tower, Westminster 56
Jewry Wall, Leicester 95
Jordan Hill Roman Temple, Weymouth 44

Kempley: St Mary's Church 54
Kenilworth Castle 144
Kenwood 57
King Charles's Castle 83
King Doniert's Stone, St Cleer 26
King James's and Landport Gates,
  Portsmouth 71
Kingston Russell Stone Circle 44
Kingswood Abbey Gatehouse 53
Kirby Hall 104
Kirby Muxloe Castle 95
Kirkham House, Paignton 40
Kirkham Priory 112
Kit's Coty House and Little Kit's Coty
  House 87
Knights Templar Church, Dover 86
Knowlton Church and Earthworks 44

Landguard Fort, Felixstowe 134
Lanercost Priory 32
Langley Chapel 123
Launceston Castle 26
Leahill Turret 64

Leicester: Jewry Wall 95
Leigh Court Barn 74
Leiston Abbey 134
Letocetum (Wall Roman Site) 132
Lexden Earthworks and Bluebottle Grove,
  Colchester 49
Lilleshall Abbey 124
Lincoln: Bishop's Palace 96
Lindisfarne Priory 108
Lindsey: St James's Chapel 135
Little Kit's Coty House 87
London Wall, Tower Hill 58
Longthorpe Tower 20
Longtown Castle 74
Ludgershall Castle and Cross 148
Lullingstone Roman Villa 87
Lyddington Bede House 95
Lydford Castles and Saxon Town 41

Maiden Castle 44
Maison Dieu, Ospringe 88
Manaton: Hound Tor Deserted Medieval
  Village 39
Marble Hill House 58
Marmion Tower 112
Mattersey Priory 117
Mayburgh Earthwork 33
Meare Fish House 128
Medieval Merchant's House,
  Southampton 69
Merrivale Prehistoric Settlement 40
Middleham Castle 113
Milton Chantry, Gravesend 88
Minster Lovell Hall and Dovecote 119
Mistley Towers 49
Mitchell's Fold Stone Circle 124
Monk Bretton Priory 130
Moreton Corbet Castle 124
Mortimer's Cross Water Mill 75
Moulton Packhorse Bridge 135
Mount Batten Tower 41
Mount Grace Priory 113
Muchelney Abbey 128

Netheravon Dovecote 148
Netley Abbey 70
Nine Ladies Stone Circle 37
Nine Stones, The, Winterbourne Abbas 44
Norham Castle 109
North Elmham Chapel 101
North Hinksey Conduit House 120
Northington: The Grange 68

North Leigh Roman Villa 119
Norwich: Cow Tower 102
Notgrove Long Barrow 53
Nunney Castle 128
Nympsfield Long Barrow 53

Odda's Chapel, Deerhurst 53
Offa's Dyke 53
Okehampton Castle 41
Old Bishop's Palace, Wolvesey 72
Old Blockhouse 83
Old Gorhambury House 76
Old Merchant's House and Row 111
    House, Great Yarmouth 101
Old Oswestry Hill Fort 124
Old Sarum 148
Old Soar Manor, Plaxtol 88
Old Wardour Castle 149
Orford Castle 135
Osborne House 81
Ospringe: Maison Dieu 88
Over Bridge 54

Paignton: Kirkham House 40
Pendennis Castle 26
Penrith Castle 33
Pevensey Castle 140
Peveril Castle 37
Pickering Castle 113
Piel Castle 33
Piercebridge Roman Bridge 114
Pike Hill Signal Tower 64
Piper Sike Turret 64
Planetrees Roman Wall 64
Plaxtol: Old Soar Manor 88
Plymouth: Royal Citadel 42
Poltross Burn Milecastle 64
Portchester Castle 70
Porth Hellick Down Burial Chamber 83
Portland Castle 45
Portsmouth: Garrison Church 70
Portsmouth: King James's and Landport
    Gates 71
Prior's Hall Barn, Widdington 50
Prudhoe Castle 109
Pyx Chamber, Westminster Abbey 59

Ranger's House 58
Ravenglass: Roman Bath House 33
Reculver Towers and Roman Fort 89
Restormel Castle 27
Richborough Castle 89
Richborough Roman Amphitheatre 89

Richmond Castle 114
Rievaulx Abbey 114
Roche Abbey 130
Rochester Castle 89
Rochester: Temple Manor 91
Rodmarton: Windmill Tump Long
    Barrow 54
Rotherwas Chapel 75
Row 111 House, Great Yarmouth 101
Royal Citadel, Plymouth 42
Royal Oak, Boscobel House 122
Rufford Abbey 117
Rushton Triangular Lodge 104
Rycote Chapel 120

St Albans: Roman Wall 76
St Augustine's Abbey, Canterbury 90
St Augustine's Cross, Ebbsfleet 90
St Botolph's Priory, Colchester 49
St Breock Downs Monolith 27
St Briavel's Castle 54
St Buryan: Tregiffian Burial Chamber 28
St Catherine's Castle, Fowey 27
St Catherine's Chapel, Abbotsbury 45
St Catherine's Oratory 80
St Cleer: King Doniert's Stone 26
St Cleer: Trethevy Quoit 28
St James's Chapel, Lindsey 135
St John's Abbey Gate, Colchester 49
St John's Commandery, Swingfield 90
St Just: Ballowall Barrow 25
St Leonard's Tower, West Malling 90
St Mary's Church, Kempley 54
St Mary's Church, Studley Royal 115
St Mawes Castle 27
St Olave's Priory 102
St Paul's Monastery and Bede Museum,
    Jarrow 142
St Peter's Church, Barton-upon-
    Humber 78
Salley Abbey 93
Sanctuary, The, Overton Hill, Avebury 150
Sandbach Crosses 22
Saxtead Green Post Mill 135
Scarborough Castle 114
Sewingshields Wall, Turrets and
    Milecastle 65
Shap Abbey 33
Sherborne Old Castle 45
Sibsey Trader Windmill 97
Silbury Hill 150
Silchester Roman City Wall 71

INDEX

Sir Bevil Grenville's Monument 15
Skipsea Castle 78
Southampton: Medieval Merchant's
    House 69
Spofforth Castle 115
Stanton Drew Stone Circles and Cove 15
Stanton Moor: Nine Ladies Stone
    Circle 37
Stanwick Iron Age Fortifications 115
Steeton Hall Gateway 115
Stokesay Castle 124
Stonehenge 149
Stoney Littleton Long Barrow 15
Stott Park Bobbin Mill 34
Studley Royal: St Mary's Church 115
Sutton Scarsdale Hall 37
Sutton Valence Castle 90
Swingfield: St John's Commandery 90

Tattershall College 97
Temple Church, Bristol 14
Temple Manor, Rochester 91
Thetford: Church of the Holy
    Sepulchre 102
Thetford Priory 102
Thetford Warren Lodge 102
Thornton Abbey 78
Tilbury Fort 50
Tintagel Castle 28
Titchfield Abbey 72
Totnes Castle 42
Tregiffian Burial Chamber, St Buryan 28
Trethevy Quoit, St Cleer 28
Tynemouth and Castle Priory 142

Uffington Castle, White Horse and Dragon
    Hill 120
Uley Long Barrow 54
Upnor Castle 91
Upper Plym Valley 42

Vindolanda Fort 65

Wall Roman Site (Letocetum) 132
Walltown Crags Wall and Turret 65
Walmer Castle 91
Waltham Abbey Gatehouse and Bridge 50
Warkworth Castle and Hermitage 109
Warton Old Rectory 93
Waverley Abbey 137
Wayland's Smithy 120
Weeting Castle 102

Wenlock Priory 125
Western Heights 86
West Kennet Avenue, Avebury 150
West Kennet Long Barrow 150
West Malling: St Leonard's Tower 90
Westminster Abbey Chapter House, Pyx
    Chamber and Abbey Museum 59
Westminster: Jewel Tower 56
Wetheral Priory Gatehouse 34
Weymouth: Jordan Hill Roman Temple 44
Whalley Abbey Gatehouse 93
Wharram Percy Church and Deserted
    Medieval Village 116
Wheeldale Roman Road 115
Whitby Abbey 116
White Horse, Uffington 120
White Ladies Priory 125
Widdington: Prior's Hall Barn 50
Willowford Bridge Abutment 65
Winchester Palace 58
Windmill Hill 151
Windmill Tump Long Barrow,
    Rodmarton 54
Winshields Wall and Milecastle 65
Winterbourne Abbas: The Nine Stones 44
Winterbourne Poor Lot Barrows 45
Witley Court 75
Wolvesey: Old Bishop's Palace 72
Woodhenge 151
Wrest Park House and Gardens 17
Wroxeter Roman City 125

Yarmouth Castle 81
Yarn Market, Dunster 127
York: Clifford's Tower 111

COVENANTS

If you are interested in covenanting your membership or paying your subscription by Direct Debit, simply write your membership number in the box provided, complete the relevant sections of the form, and return it to: ENGLISH HERITAGE MEMBERSHIP DEPARTMENT, PO BOX 1BB, LONDON W1A 1BB.

MEMBERSHIP NUMBER

DEED OF COVENANT

I (FULL NAME IN CAPITALS)	
OF (ADDRESS)	
	POSTCODE

COVENANT with ENGLISH HERITAGE that for 4 years or during my lifetime (whichever period shall be shorter) I will pay to them every year such a sum as, after deduction of income tax at the basic rate for the time being in force, amounts to the equivalent of the annual membership subscription payable to English Heritage as at the date on which payment is due.

SIGNED AND DELIVERED		DATE	
WITNESS'S SIGNATURE		WITNESS'S NAME	
ADDRESS			
		POSTCODE	

Source code 0013

DIRECT DEBIT INSTRUCTION

NAME OF ACCOUNT HOLDER(S)	
BANK ACCOUNT NO.	BANK SORT CODE

Prior to any subscription increase, we undertake to write to you well in advance of processing the debit. You can cancel this authority at any time by instructing your bank and notifying us. Banks may decline to accept instructions to charge Direct Debits to certain types of accounts other than current accounts.

BANK	
BRANCH ADDRESS	
	POSTCODE

I/We instruct you to pay Direct Debits from my/our account at the request of English Heritage. The amounts are variable and may be debited on various dates.
I/We understand that English Heritage may change the amounts and dates only after giving me/us prior notice.
I/We will inform the bank in writing if I/we wish to cancel this instruction.
I/We understand that if any Direct Debit is paid which breaks the terms of the instruction the bank will make a refund.

SIGNATURE(S)		DATE	

Instruction to Bank:
Please quote the following reference:

Originators Identification No. 940123

157

How to become a member of English Heritage

Taking out membership of English Heritage helps us to protect and repair England's historic environment whilst giving you the freedom to visit all of our 350 properties listed in this Guide absolutely free.

All you have to do is complete the form on the opposite page and return it to us. There are a range of different categories all representing excellent value for money, and you choose how you wish to pay: by cheque, credit card or direct debit.

Please also consider covenanting your subscription. This allows us to reclaim from the Inland Revenue the basic rate of income tax that you have paid on the cost of your subscription. So the value of your subscription actually increases by 33% — without any extra cost to you.

All you have to do is agree to remain a member for the next four years and then, in the presence of a witness, sign and date the Deed of Covenant form on page 157. Please also consider filling in the Direct Debit instruction on the same page. This will not only help you avoid any worries about forgetting to pay your subscription over this period, but will save us money on administration costs.

Then simply return your completed forms to: English Heritage Membership Department, PO Box 1BB, London W1A 1BB.

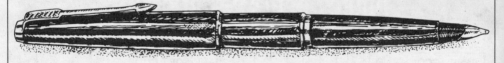

How to renew your Membership

If you are already a member of English Heritage please do not complete the form on page 159. We will automatically remind you when it is time to renew your membership by mailing you with the details.

However, you can make your subscription work even harder at no extra cost to you by completing the Deed of Covenant and Direct Debit forms on page 157 and returning them to us at the above address.

MEMBERSHIP APPLICATION FORM

Please choose the membership category you prefer and then fill in the application form, preferably with the Deed of Covenant and Direct Debiting Instruction on page 157 as well, IN BLOCK CAPITALS. Please allow 28 days for delivery.

N.B. Do not use this form for renewing your membership as we will automatically send you new cards together with an invoice for payment.

Send the complete form, along with your payment, to: English Heritage Membership Department, PO Box 1BB, London W1A 1BB.

(These prices are effective until 31st March 1993.)

✂

All applicants to complete this section	Source Code: 0013

YOUR PERSONAL DETAILS

TITLE	INITIALS	SURNAME

ADDRESS

	POSTCODE	

DATE OF BIRTH IF UNDER 21	

ADDITIONAL ADULT MEMBER AT SAME ADDRESS

TITLE	INITIALS	SURNAME

FAMILY MEMBERS UNDER 21 (not required for children under 5)

Please attach a separate list if you wish to enrol more than three children.

TITLE	INITIALS	SURNAME

DATE OF BIRTH

TITLE	INITIALS	SURNAME

DATE OF BIRTH

TITLE	INITIALS	SURNAME

DATE OF BIRTH

TWELVE MONTH MEMBERSHIPS

IND	Adult: £15.00	£ :
IND2	Two Adults at the same address: £25.00	£ :
FG	Family: £30.00 for two parents and all children over 5 and under 21. Each member receives an individual card.	£ :
SP	Single Parent Family: £17.00 for one parent and all children over 5 and under 21 years.	£ :
SNRC	Senior Citizen: £10.50 for people aged 60 and over.	£ :
SNR2	Two Senior Citizens at the same address: £17.50	£ :
ISC	Adult & Senior Citizen at the same address: £22.50	£ :
STUD	Young Person: £10.50 for people from 16–20 years.	£ :
JNR	Junior: £7.00 for the under 16's including membership of KEEP	£ :

LIFE MEMBERSHIPS

INDL	Individual life: £300.00. This entitles a member to bring a guest at no extra charge.	£ :
JNTL	Joint life: £375.00 for husband and wife, each receiving their own card. Up to four accompanying children under 16 years also admitted.	£ :
SNRL	Senior Citizen life: £190.00 available to anyone aged 60 years and over. Entitles a member to bring a guest at no extra charge.	£ :
JNSL	Joint Senior Citizen life: £240.00 for husband and wife aged 60 years and over each receiving their own card. Up to four accompanying children under 16 years also admitted.	£ :

Complete this section if paying by credit card

PLEASE TICK	ACCESS	VISA	AMEX

CARD NUMBER			

NAME	EXPIRY DATE

We may arrange for you to receive information on products or services we think may be of interest to you. If you do not wish to receive these please tick the box. ☐

159